Stefan Luckner / Jan Schröder / Christian Slamka et al.

Prediction Markets

GABLER RESEARCH

Stefan Luckner / Jan Schröder
Christian Slamka / Markus Franke
Andreas Geyer-Schulz / Bernd Skiera
Martin Spann / Christof Weinhardt

Prediction Markets

Fundamentals, Designs,
and Applications

GABLER

RESEARCH

Bibliographic information published by the Deutsche Nationalbibliothek
The Deutsche Nationalbibliothek lists this publication in the Deutsche Nationalbibliografie; detailed bibliographic data are available in the Internet at http://dnb.d-nb.de.

1st Edition 2012

Editorial Office: Ute Wrasmann | Nicole Schweitzer

Gabler Verlag is a brand of Springer Fachmedien.
Springer Fachmedien is part of Springer Science+Business Media.
www.gabler.de

Cover design: KünkelLopka Medienentwicklung, Heidelberg
Printed on acid-free paper

ISBN 978-3-8349-3358-4

Preface

Accurate predictions are essential in many areas such as corporate decision making, weather forecasting and technology forecasting. Prediction markets are a promising approach for predicting uncertain future events and developments. They have done well in every known comparison with other forecasting methods. Prediction markets help to aggregate information and gain a better understanding of the future by collecting knowledge of as many people as possible. In prediction markets contracts whose payoff depends on uncertain future events are traded. Traders buy and sell contracts based on their expectations regarding the likelihood of future events. Trading prices thus reflect the traders' aggregated expectations on the outcome of uncertain future events and can be used to predict the likelihood of these events.

This book demonstrates that markets are accurate predictors beyond the field of political stock markets. Results from several empirical studies reported in this work demonstrate the importance of designing such markets properly in order to derive valuable predictions. Therefore, our findings are valuable for designing future prediction markets.

This work on prediction markets was funded by the German Federal Ministry for Education and Research (BMBF) under grant number 01HQ0522. We are grateful for this funding and strongly believe that prediction markets will continue to raise interest in academia as well as in industry.

The authors

Table of Contents

List of Figures

List of Abbreviations

CA	Call auction
CDA	Continuous Double Auction
DPM	Dynamic pari-mutuel market
DV	Deposit value
FIFA	Fédération Internationale de Football Association
FP	Fixed payment
GDP	Gross Domestic Product
HP	Hewlett-Packard
HSX	Hollywood Stock Exchange
IEM	Iowa Electronic Markets
MM	Market maker
MSR	Market scoring rule
PSM	Political Stock Market
RO	Rank-order tournament
UBC	University of British Columbia

List of Tables

1. Introduction

Uncertainty and doubt are seen to be major challenges for management in the 21st century (Nohria and Stewart, 2006). Considering the environment in which organizations are acting today, this is not surprising: Increasing speed of innovation and thus shorter product life cycles as well as the globalization of markets make our world increasingly complex and unpredictable. Hence, for organizations it is more important than ever to develop foresight capabilities to better foresee future developments, trends, potentials, challenges, and risks (van Bruggen et al., 2006).

Predicting the future is an integral part of corporate decision making. Inaccurate or delayed predictions can result in substantial costs for a company. Improving foresight capabilities, on the other hand, helps to strengthen the position of a company in global competition. Most business challenges related to, for example, demand forecasting and new product development require information which is dispersed among many people (Soukhoroukova et al., 2010). However, these people cannot be easily identified in most cases. But more and more companies recognize the potential of collective intelligence and try to leverage the *wisdom of crowds*[1] through technologies such as wikis, blogs, or reputational systems. All of these technologies help to aggregate information and gain a better understanding of the future by collecting knowledge of as many people as possible.

1.1. Motivation

Over the last couple of years, interest in prediction markets, also called information markets (Hahn and Tetlock, 2006) or virtual stock markets (Spann and Skiera, 2003) as a forecasting method has continuously increased in the scientific world and in industry. With regard to information *markets* play a triple role: they provide incentives for information revelation, and the market mechanism provides ways for information revelation and aggregation So far, prediction markets have done well in every known comparison with other forecasting methods (Hanson, 2006). Racetrack odds beat horse experts consistently (Figlewski, 1979), orange juice futures have proven more accurate than the National Weather Service of the US Department of Commerce (Roll, 1984), and stock prices determined the company responsible for the explosion of the Challenger

[1] Surowiecki (2004) created public interest in collective intelligence with his bestselling book "The Wisdom of Crowds".

spacecraft within 13 minutes – four months before a panel of experts published its official report (Maloney and Mulherin, 2003). Whereas information aggregation is only a byproduct of most traditional markets, prediction markets are set up with the explicit purpose of soliciting information. Engineered carefully, prediction markets can directly guide decision making.

The basic idea of prediction markets is to trade contracts whose payoff depends on the outcome of uncertain future events. Although the final payoffs of the contracts are unknown during the trading period, rational traders should sell contracts if they consider them to be overvalued and buy contracts if they consider them to be undervalued (Glosten and Milgrom, 1985). Until the outcome is finally known, the trading prices reflect the traders' aggregated beliefs about the likelihood of the future events (Spann and Skiera, 2003). In efficient markets, all the available information is reflected in the trading prices at any time (Fama, 1970a, Fama, 1991).

Examples of prediction markets that are open to the public include the Iowa Electronic Markets[2], the Political Stock Market PSM[3], TradeSports[4], the Hollywood Stock Exchange[5], and STOCCER[6]. Several major companies such as Hewlett-Packard, Google, or Microsoft are also using internal prediction markets for company-specific predictions. The results of recent studies on these prediction markets are encouraging. One of the main reasons for their dissemination is that they have shown a high prediction accuracy compared to traditional forecasting methods such as polls, expert predictions, or surveys (Berg et al., 2001, Servan-Schreiber et al., 2004, Spann and Skiera, 2003). Good performance has also been demonstrated in corporate environments (Chen and Plott, 2002, Ortner, 2000, Plott, 2000). Beyond prediction accuracy, markets also provide considerable advantages in terms of continuous forecasting, participation, and cost efficiency compared to other widespread forecasting methods.

Continuous scanning of ongoing developments as an input to strategic planning may be difficult to implement with traditional forecasting methods such as brainstorming techniques, expert groups, Delphi studies, and scenario workshops. The results of such approaches usually have to be manually analyzed, evaluated, and summarized. All of this

[2] http://www.biz.uiowa.edu/iem
[3] http://psm.em.uni-karlsruhe.de
[4] http://www.tradesports.com
[5] http://www.hsx.com
[6] http://www.stoccer.com

has to be performed at a certain point in time. In contrast, all the traders' information is aggregated by the price mechanism of a prediction market. This has two positive effects: First, the information aggregation by the price mechanism reduces the workload compared to traditional forecasting methods. Second, the price mechanism ensures that trading prices continuously reflect the totality of previously revealed knowledge and immediately respond to new information (Hanson, 1999). This means that information aggregated via prediction markets is available in the market and always up-to-date (Berg et al., 2003).

Concerning participation in foresight studies, it is a well-known problem that people generally refuse to participate or drop out early due to other commitments they consider more important (Cuhls, 2003). Therefore, it makes sense to provide incentives for participation. With proper incentive schemes traders do not necessarily state their individual preferences but their true beliefs (van Bruggen et al., 2006). Prediction markets allow for rather sophisticated incentive schemes as traders can be rewarded based on their performance, i.e. the quality of their contributions. This can happen in different ways. The market operator can for instance award prizes or money to the best traders or traders can be asked for investing some of their own money in a market. Yet, it is sometimes not even essential to provide monetary incentives or prizes to motivate participation. Prediction markets have also shown to perform well without providing any monetary incentives, e.g. by publicly announcing a ranking based on the traders' success in the market (Christiansen, 2007).

The implementation of a foresight activity is often restricted due to tight budget constraints and other resource limitations (Salo and Cuhls, 2003, Clar, 2003). As described above, the information aggregation process in prediction markets is carried out via the price mechanism and does not require any manual intervention. Prediction markets are highly scalable as the workload of the operators is almost independent from the number of traders and the time horizon (Chan et al., 2002). Furthermore, the hardware costs for running a market are negligible once the market platform has been designed and developed (Spann et al., 2009).

To sum up, evidence so far suggests that prediction markets are at least as accurate as traditional forecasting methods. Furthermore, they provide considerable advantages in terms of continuous forecasting, participation and information revelation as well as scalability and cost efficiency. This also explains why prediction markets currently receive a lot of attention in research.

First of all, this work discusses the key design elements of prediction markets which are crucial for their successful implementation. Results from several empirical studies reported in this work demonstrate the importance of designing such markets properly in order to derive valuable predictions. Moreover, we present results from earlier research and several field experiments to show that prediction markets have immense predictive power and that they are useful in a broad field of applications. To give just a few examples, such markets successfully were applied for predicting the outcome of sports events or political elections, for natural resource management, for predicting economic indicators, and for assessing new products or services.

1.2. Overview and Structure

This book at hand is structured into five chapters. After the introduction in Chapter 1 to this book, Chapter 2 gives a definition of prediction markets and explains their operational principle as well as their theoretical foundations. Chapter 3 discusses the key design elements of prediction markets which have to be considered by market engineers. Several empirical studies are used to demonstrate the impact of market design on the performance of such markets. To give an example, we study the impact of different incentive schemes on prediction accuracy. We elaborate on the question whether or not prediction markets with performance-related incentives perform better than markets with flat payments and how these performance-related incentives should be designed. This problem is of special interest when traders need to get paid for taking part in a prediction market, e.g., in the case of an internal market for company-specific predictions. The results show that the highest correlation between the outcome and trading prices is found in case of a rank-order tournament where traders are paid depending on their ordinal rank in a group of traders. Thus, tournaments with a handful of big winners winning big prizes work well. Somewhat surprisingly, the rank-order tournament even seems to beat the incentive scheme where the traders' payments are based linearly on their return in the market.

Subsequently, Chapter 4 presents previous fields of application of prediction markets and discusses several field experiments in more detail. We start with a description of a 2006 FIFA World Cup prediction market called STOCCER. The FIFA World Cup 2006 itself, the contracts that were traded, the trading mechanisms, the incentive schemes, the group of traders, as well as the software platform are described in detail. We examine the accuracy of prediction markets for predicting the outcomes of soccer matches during the FIFA World Cup 2006. The results show that play money prediction markets outperform a random predictor and forecasts that are based on historic data about the success of national soccer teams. Moreover, prediction markets are on a level with betting odds from professional bookmakers which are known to be very accurate. Beyond the comparison of prediction accuracy, we also investigate whether pure arbitrage opportunities existed in these markets and whether traders try to exploit illiquidity by taking on the role of market makers in prediction markets. Beyond STOCCER, we also present the political stock market PSM and the The Australian Knowledge eXchange AKX. At the end of the chapter we give an outlook on how prediction markets can be used to generate and evaluate innovative products and services.

Chapter 5 summarizes this work and proposes promising future fields of application for prediction markets.

2. Fundamentals of Prediction Markets

After a short history of prediction markets in Section 2.1, we define prediction markets as markets that run for "the primary purpose of aggregating information so that market prices forecast future events" (Berg and Rietz, 2003) in Section 2.2. The theoretic foundations of prediction markets are found in Hayek's analysis of market-based economies and in the rose of information in Fama's efficient market hypothesis in Section 2.3. The interaction between incentives for trade information revelation by trading transactions and the resulting adaption of prices is illustrated by a hands-on example in Section 2.4 on the operational principle of prediction markets.

2.1. History

Throughout history business people have always tried to forecast the future to improve the performance of their companies. Commodity futures can be traced back to the Middle Ages when farmers and merchants faced the risk of price changes as a result of weather conditions or wars. In recent years, a relatively new approach for information aggregation has gained importance in the area of forecasting, namely prediction markets. Prediction markets bring a group of participants together and let them trade contracts whose payoff depends on the outcome of uncertain future events. The contracts thus represent a bet on the outcome of those future events. Once the outcome is known traders receive a cash payment in exchange for the contracts they hold.

Several studies describe how such markets have been applied for predicting future events or developments in the field of politics (Forsythe et al., 1992), sports (Luckner et al., 2007, Luckner, 2007, Spann and Skiera, 2009), medicine (Polgreen et al., 2007), entertainment (Pennock et al., 2000), or economy (Spann and Skiera, 2003). Moreover, companies like Siemens or Hewlett-Packard have employed prediction markets in order to improve their decision making (Chen and Plott, 2002, Ortner, 1997).

2.2. Definition

In the academic literature, there is no universal definition of the term "prediction market". Alternative terms used for the same concept include information markets, decision markets, idea futures, forecasting markets, artificial markets, electronic markets, and virtual stock markets. The definition of prediction markets used in this work is based on Berg et al. (Berg and Rietz, 2003, Berg et al., 2003). According to this definition, prediction markets are defined as markets that are run for "the primary purpose of aggregating information so that market prices forecast future events" (Berg and Rietz, 2003, p. 3). Moreover, prediction markets can also serve as decision support systems by providing information about the current situation or by evaluating effects of decisions over time (Berg and Rietz, 2003, Hanson, 1999).

Although prediction markets that are designed for information aggregation and revelation are at the focus of this work, the distinction between these markets and stock markets or betting markets can become fuzzy. In contrast to prediction markets, however, stock markets are established with the primary purpose of allocating resources, trading risk, and raising capital. Information aggregation is only a pleasant byproduct of stock markets while prediction markets are usually not substantial enough in size to allow for a considerable extent of risk sharing even though they may take on this role as interest and depth increase (Wolfers and Zitzewitz, 2004). Whereas contracts in stock markets are based on an underlying real asset, prediction markets create contracts which are linked to the outcomes of events but do not have any value by themselves. Betting markets, on the other hand, are first and foremost set up for entertainment and tend to trade risk that is intrinsically enjoyable. Thus, the primary purpose of a market can probably be seen as the main distinctive feature between prediction markets, betting markets, and stock markets.

2.3. Theoretical Foundations

The idea that trading mechanisms could be used to aggregate information dispersed among traders traces back to Hayek (Hayek, 1945). Hayek argued that planners in centrally-planned economies do not have enough information to calculate an optimal solution for resource allocation since central planners need information about all available resources and the preferences of people. He claimed that an efficient distribution of resources can only be maintained through the use of price signals in open markets. Accordingly, Hayek hypothesized that markets are the most efficient instrument to aggregate all the dispersed information of traders. Prices thus help to coordinate the separate actions of people.

"While the exact method by which information gets into the market is unknown" (Plott, 2000, p. 8), both theoretical and empirical research have found evidence that this process takes place. The efficient market hypothesis formulated by Eugene Fama states that stock "prices at any time 'fully reflect' all available information" (Fama, 1970b, p. 383). This implies that no additionally available information can be combined with efficient prices to improve the prediction accuracy of a market. Moreover, in financial markets it is impossible to consistently outperform the market by using any information that the market already knows. There are three common forms of market efficiency (Jensen, 1978). While the weak form efficient market hypothesis asserts that prices reflect all information contained in historic prices of the market, the semi-strong form efficient market hypothesis asserts that prices reflect all publicly available information. Of course, this also includes the past history of prices. Finally, the strong form efficient market hypothesis suggests that all relevant information known to anyone is reflected by the prices. The semi-strong form of the efficient market hypothesis is the accepted paradigm whereas there is evidence inconsistent with the strong form (Jensen, 1978).

Much of the enthusiasm for prediction markets derives from the efficient markets hypothesis due to the fact that contract prices reflect all information on the corresponding future event in an efficient prediction market and thus are the best predictor of future events. Information aggregation occurs when people can infer something from observing other traders' believes and add that information to their own prior beliefs until there is a common knowledge equilibrium (McKelvey and Page, 1990).

Experimental research has tested the information aggregating properties of markets (e.g. Plott, 2000, Plott and Sunder, 1982, Plott and Sunder, 1988). In an experiment subjects traded contracts which paid 200 if the state was Y and 400 if the state was X with probabilities of 0.75 and 0.25. During so called informed states, some insiders knew the state of the world. Prices in these markets converged to the correct value when insiders were present and for the most part to the expected value of 250 if none of the traders were insiders. Thus, these markets were able to collect and broadcast information held by some of the traders (Plott, 2000).

In real-world scenarios, however, knowledge is usually dispersed among traders. Consequently, the question arises whether markets can aggregate this dispersed information. Therefore, in another experiment every subject was given partial, private information. Collectively, the traders had almost perfect information regarding the correct state. The results show that information aggregation did also occur in this case (Plott, 2000).

2.4. Operational Principle

Prediction markets are a new form of financial markets where contracts whose payoff depends on the outcomes of uncertain future events are traded. Traders buy and sell contracts based on their expectations regarding the likelihood of future events. Trading prices thus reflect the traders' aggregated expectations on the outcome of uncertain future events and can be used to predict the likelihood of these events. The basic idea is that according to the efficient market hypothesis (Fama, 1970b) trading prices reflect all available information and the price mechanism serves as a means of aggregating the traders' collective expectations (Spann and Skiera, 2003).

An example for the operational principle of prediction markets is shown in Figure 1. Suppose that the board of directors of a small deluxe car manufacturer needs reliable sales forecasts to adapt operational processes and minimize operational costs. All employees who have access to relevant information are given an initial endowment and access to the prediction market. Several contracts can be traded on this market. For example, the contract "500-600 cars in 2008" pays off 100 € if the company actually sells 500 to 600 cars in 2008; otherwise the pay-off is 0 €.

Assume that at a certain point in time the contract trades at a price of 45 €. In this case the trading price denotes that the probability that the car manufacturer will sell 500 to 600 cars in 2008 is assumed to be 45%. If a trader believes that the likelihood of selling 500 to 600 cars in 2008 is 70%, he should buy (sell) contracts for any price lower (higher) than 70 €. Thus, the trader would buy contracts at a price of 45 €.

As can be seen in this example a trader's dissent from the aggregated expectation would provoke a transaction and consequently usually change the trading prices. The trading mechanism automatically executes matching orders, i.e. buy and sell orders that are overlapping or placed at the same price. It is natural to assume that the higher a trader considers the probability of an event, the higher is both his reluctance to sell and his willingness to pay. Hence, the trading price gives some indication of how likely the traders as a group consider the event to occur. In this way, the trading price of the contract "500-600 cars in 2008" should reflect all the traders' information and can thus be interpreted as the probability of selling 500 to 600 cars in 2008.

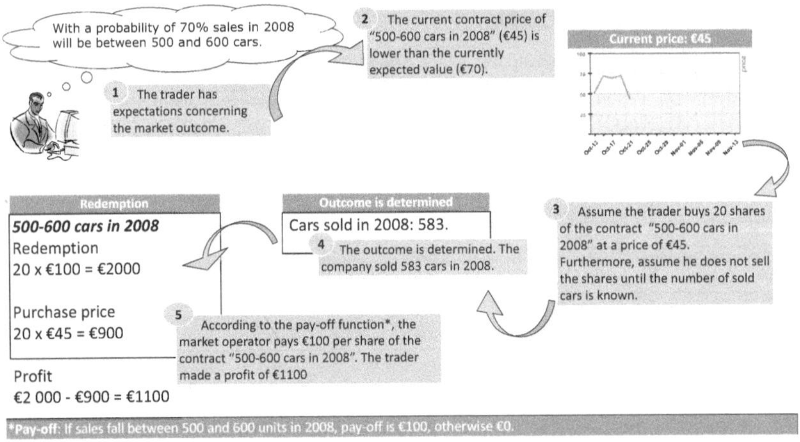

Figure 1: Operational principle of prediction markets

Depending on their performance, traders can either win or lose money. In the above-mentioned example, the trader bought 20 contracts "500-600 cars in 2008" at a price of 45 € and finally received a payment of 100 € per contract since the company indeed sold between 500 and 600 cars in 2008. Therefore, prediction markets motivate participation and well-designed incentive schemes motivate traders to reveal their beliefs instead of their preferences. To give an example, even an enthusiastic supporter of a deluxe car among the employees of the above-mentioned car manufacturer would rather not try to boost the sales forecasts of his favorite car since he would lose money in case he was overestimating sales figures.

3. Key Design Elements of Prediction Markets

Before studying more advanced applications of prediction markets, it is necessary to gain a basic understanding of their key design elements. Like any market, prediction markets have to be designed and implemented very carefully in order to ensure that they are suitable for aggregating traders' information (Weinhardt et al., 2003, Weinhardt et al., 2006a). The key design elements comprise the specification of *contracts* traded in a prediction market, the *trading mechanism*, and the *incentives* provided to ensure information revelation (Spann and Skiera, 2003). Moreover, diversity of information is required in order to provide a basis for trading (Wolfers and Zitzewitz, 2004). Heterogeneous expectations about the future among traders are desirable and the selection of *traders* is thus also considered a key design issue (Tziralis and Tatsiopoulos, 2007b). The following subsections describe these design elements in more detail.

3.1. Contracts

One of the most crucial first questions a PM initiator has to answer is how the stocks' underlying contracts are defined. In general, we can say that a contract defines how an outcome of an event to be forecasted is mapped to the payoff, or in other words, how the final values of stocks after the closing of the markets are specified.

Depending on the forecasting goal, a PM designer can choose from different contract types. Each payoff type corresponds to a different prediction. Wolfers and Zitzewitz ((2004) distinguish between contracts of the following type:

1) Winner-takes-all contracts
2) Linear or index contracts
3) Spread contracts.

An example for each of these contracts types is shown in Table 1. For an alternative classification see (Spann and Skiera, 2003). This list is not exhaustive, as there are different types of contracts to be found, as e.g. in STOCCER. However, most of these types build up on these basic types.

Contract type	Example	Payoff	Prediction of
Winner-takes all	"Product X will beat last year's sales"	\$100 if event happens, else \$0.	Probability of event to occur
Linear or index	"Percentage of total market share of product X next year"	\$1 for every underlying base value point	Mean value of outcome
Spread	"Product X's sales next year" expressed by "Product X's sales will raise more than y % next year"	Contract costs certain fixed amount. Pays off at twice the value, if spread is true, else \$0.	Median value of outcome.

Table 1: Contract types (table on the basis of (Wolfers and Zitzewitz, 2004))

The most common contract type is the "winner-takes-all" type. In this case, the payoff is \$100 (or \$1), if the underlying event happens, and \$0, if it does not. It has been shown empirically (e.g. Cowgill et al., 2008) as well as theoretically (Wolfers and Zitzewitz, 2006) that current prices reflect the probability of an event to happen, expressing the aggregated traders' beliefs about the outcome. While the example in Table 1 is expressed as single stock, in winner-takes-all markets several stocks with a different outcome of a common underlying event can be constructed. In sports, for instance, a number of teams may play in one league, but only one team will definitely win the championships. In order to predict the winner of the championships, a PM initiator would create one stock per team and define each stock's payoff as \$100 if the corresponding team wins the championships, and \$0, if it does not. As the stock's current prices during the trading time reflect the probabilities of the corresponding teams to win the championships, the sum of all stock prices should be exactly \$100.

A second common contract type is the "linear" or "index" type. In the Iowa Electronic Markets, this type is also referred to as "vote-share" in the special context of presidential elections (Berg et al., 2003). As opposed to the winner-takes-all type, in linear-type markets, any (positive) number can be assigned as payoff, such as the sales of product X next year and possibly divided by a constant such as 1,000,000. Thus for instance, sales of \$30,000,000 in a given year for product X would result in a payoff of \$30,000,000 / 1,000,000 = \$30. As it can easily be seen, a current trading price of linear stock corresponds to the mean aggregated traders' beliefs about the outcome.

The last type, "spread", is usually less frequent to be seen as its interpretation is not as straight forward as before. Consider an example where the number of scored goals of a team should be predicted. While the mean market expectation of the number of scored goals in this case can be predicted with the linear type, the spread type can predict the median expectations of all traders. This is accomplished defining the contract as "Pays even money if the number of scored goals is greater than y". In contrast to the previous two types where the stock price depending on supply and demand changes for this contract, the stock price is fixed at some number, e.g. $1. However, the number y changes depending on supply and demand. The contract pays $2, if the number of scored goals is greater than y, and $0, if the number is below or equal y. As it is clear now, by specifying the segregation point by trading, half of the bets are below y and half of the bets are greater than y, and thus, the median expectation of the outcome is predicted by the market.

Restrictions on the type of contracts do not only have to arise from the forecasting goal, but also from the market structure, possibly eliminating one of the pure contract types. E.g., a PM operator has to determine how shares are initiated to the market. While this is possible by using automated market makers (see next subsection) or an initial endowment with shares for each trader, many PMs such as the IEM use so-called unit portfolios. A PM operator can offer unit portfolios containing a fixed set of shares for sale as well as for purchase for a fixed price. This price is identical to the sum of payoffs of all shares in the portfolio. Thus, buying and selling the portfolio is free of risk for the operator and establishes a way to introduce shares to the market. However, because the sum of the payoffs must be fixed and known in advance, linear stocks cannot be traded. However, a "linear" stock can be simulated by splitting a linear range up in intervals and creating winner-takes-all stocks (Spann and Skiera, 2003). For instance: "Sales will be below $10m", "Sales will be between $10m and $20m" and "Sales will be more than $20m".

Beyond the formal specification of the contracts, some important practical considerations have to be made as well concerning unexpected incidents. In this case, the rules of the PMs must make a clear statement about the further procedure with this kind of exceptions. Unexpected incidents could include:

- Occurrence of an event which has not been covered by existing contracts, i.e. contracts are not exhaustive.
- Ranges of predictions are out of range, e.g. negative numbers in case of linear markets.
- Outcomes of events cannot be observed, e.g. a sports game can be canceled.

3.2. Trading Mechanisms

Another crucial question a PM operator must decide on is which market mechanism to use, i.e. how to match demand and supply influencing the price of the shares and therewith, predictions. In earlier PMs such as the (real-money) Iowa Electronic Markets and as in most financial exchanges such as the Frankfurt Stock Exchange, a standard double auction (DA) mechanism is employed, which matches orders of sellers and buyers (see Figure 2, upper diagram).

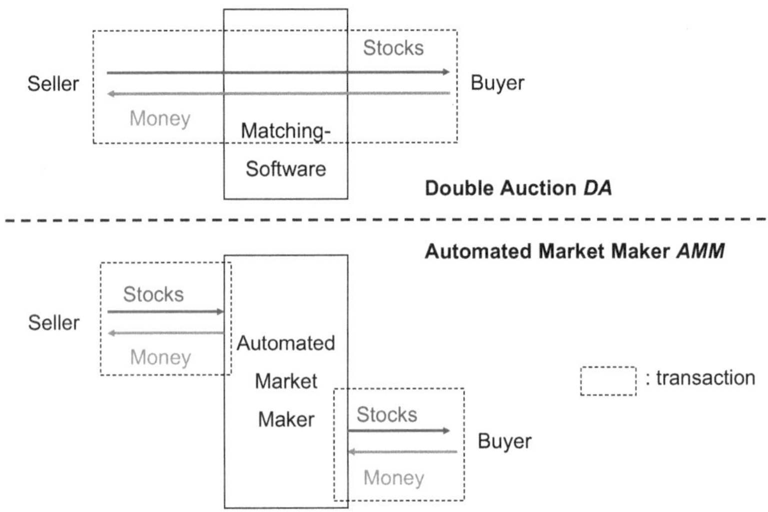

Figure 2: Functioning of a standard double auction and an automated market maker (from Slamka et al. (2009b))

However, in many, especially small, PMs, the number of traders in markets is very low or the number of stocks per trader is very high. This essentially leads to a "chicken-and-egg problem": traders are attracted to liquid markets, i.e. markets with a high trading frequency, but on the other hand, liquid markets require many traders (Pennock, 2004). Because of this illiquidity problem, in many PMs, so-called automated market makers (AMMs) are in use as a counterparty for trading. In contrast to the DA, transactions using AMMs do not occur among market participants, but between the AMM as a piece of software and participants in each buy or sell transaction (Hanson, 2003, Pennock, 2004). By providing instant buy and sell opportunities at transparent prices, participants do not have to wait for matching counteroffers to execute their trades. So far, companies such as KENFORX, Inkling, or the Hollywood Stock Exchanges are using AMMs for trading in their play-money exchanges.

Existing mechanisms and their areas of application

We describe the existing mechanisms below. Most of these explanations were adapted from Slamka et al. (2009b).

Double auctions (DAs)

In DAs, traders submit orders with a chosen fixed quantity of shares, usually with a price limit, into the order book. If no price limit is specified, the order is referred to as market order. Orders with a limit are called limit orders. If a matching order is found, then the price bid in the buy order is at least as high as the ask price of the sell order, and the order could be and is usually immediately executed. If no matching order is available, the order stays in the order book and remains there until it expires, is matched with a counteroffer, or is removed (Madhavan, 1992).

In the case of the continuous DA (CDA), which is by far the most common DA in PMs and financial markets, if a matching order is found, the order is executed immediately. Thus, trades can be executed on a continuous basis, if enough liquidity, i.e. orders, is present. This property is especially important when dealing with real-time actions, such as sports games, where the underlying true values of stock prices can rapidly change, e.g., when a goal is scored in a soccer game.

However, if the market is not liquid enough to allow for continuous trading, one possibility is to gather orders for a certain period of time, and then perform execution according to a priority rule, e.g. the principle of the highest executable volume, at given points in time. This concept is known as call auctions (CAs), and is also implemented in financial markets, such as in the hybrid trading system Xetra of the Deutsche Boerse AG.

Here, a CA is used to determine the opening price for a stock, and then a CDA is employed throughout the rest of the trading day.

DAs, CDA as well as CA, do not engage in the transaction itself, which is executed only among market participants. Thus, if carefully set-up, e.g. with unit portfolios, running DAs is essentially free of financial risk for the operator. This is probably one of the main reasons, large real-money exchanges, such as Betfair, employ a CDA in their trading system. Most prominently in academia, the IEM also make use of CDAs. On the other hand, CAs have to-date not found much attention in PMs. To our knowledge, only STOCCER has experimented with CAs during the Soccer World Championships 2006 (Geyer-Schulz et al., 2007).

Market Scoring Rules (MSR)

Market scoring rules (MSR) build upon the long-known concept of scoring rules, which has been used to evaluate a forecaster's performance (Hanson, 2003, Hanson, 2007). By being evaluated with scoring rules, forecasters are incentivized to reveal their subjectively most accurate predictions.

While with simple scoring rules forecasters give isolated one-time predictions, the basic idea of Hanson's market scoring rules (Snyder, 1978) is that forecasters give successive predictions on one particular forecasting goal by adjusting the former most current prediction. The amount this forecaster receives for his prediction is the improvement of prediction, which can be negative, if it turns out the forecaster has moved the prediction in the "wrong" direction, i.e., farther away from the actual outcome than his predecessor has forecasted. This concept of moving probability estimates can be modeled by introducing shares of underlying events which can be traded. With an underlying continuous price function, which is dependent on the particular scoring rule being used, the AMM determines the price for each share which is sold or bought. One beneficial property of MSRs is that, although markets running a MSR have to be subsidized, losses are limited, and an upper bound for losses can be determined.

Dynamic Pari-Mutuel Market

Standard pari-mutuel markets are known from e.g. horse races and are known to be able to aggregate information efficiently at one point in time (Pennock, 2004). However, they are not able to update predictions on the arrival of new information, such as news (Slamka et al., 2008). Yet in PMs, an update of the prediction as a reaction to news is a crucial feature, as the "value" of an event can be determined (Pennock, 2004). This is because participants in pari-mutuel markets are not incentivized to trade before the close of the market. The dynamic pari-mutuel market (DPM (Mangold et al., 2005)), which is e.g. applied in the Yahoo! Buzz markets (Pennock and Sami, 2007), overcomes this problem by introducing dynamic prices for shares of the final amount of money, rather than having a fixed price as with the standard mechanism. The price of a share depends, similar to the MSRs, on the number of shares in the market and on the utilized continuous price function (Soukhoroukova et al., 2009, van Bruggen et al., 2006). As in the standard pari-mutuel market, all money is redistributed over all winning shares and the price of a share does not directly correspond to actual probabilities, but has to be transformed into probabilities. As with the MSR, this mechanism has an upper bound on the losses which can occur.

Dynamic Price Adjustment (DPA)

In the LMSR and the DPM, a continuous price function exists which determines the price of a share dependent on the order quantity. The mechanism which was used in (Slamka et al., 2009b), which we will call Dynamic Price Adjustment (DPA), does not implement a continuous price function, but offers an equal buy and sell price for up to a certain maximum quantity. After the transaction, a new price is calculated depending on the last executed trades within a moving window. E.g., if a purchase occurred, the price will rise, and it will rise even more if the last transactions were also purchases, indicating an increase in the underlying true value. However, this mechanism is not arbitrage free, meaning that by skillful trading, traders could exploit the mechanism and use it as "cash cow". Thus, measures against this kind of behavior, such as a limiting buy and sell orders, have to be implemented. Another side effect is that the maximum loss of this AMM is not limited.

Hollywood Stock Exchange Mechanism (HSX)

The last mechanism presented here is employed by the Hollywood Stock Exchange (HSX), one of the biggest PMs online. The mechanism has not publicly been described in every single detail; however, the basic idea has been published in three subsequent patents (Spann and Skiera, 2003). In a certain time frame and for a specific stock, buy and sell orders are collected, comparable to call auctions in financial markets (see above), which is called the sweep period. However, they are not immediately executed. At the end of the time frame, a net-movement balance is determined, which essentially is the difference of the number of shares of buy orders minus the number of shares of sell orders. Thus, if this number is positive, demand for the stock is higher than supply, indicating a higher "true value" of the underlying stock.

Then, the net-movement balance is multiplied by a factor, resulting in the projected price movement. The price movement can potentially be attenuated by a "Virtual Specialist" function if the movement is found to be too strong. Now, the new price is calculated as the old price plus the price movement. At this point, the final buy/sell price for the orders in the elapsed time frame is calculated and the user can be informed about the final buy or sell price. Like the DPA, the HSX is not arbitrage free, and losses are not limited.

Comparison

We present a comparison of mechanisms, which is again mainly adapted from Slamka et al. (2009b), from a theoretic as well as a simulative point of view.

Theoretical comparison

Regarding general properties, it has been mentioned above that the CDA and CA do not provide for immediate and unlimited buy-/sell liquidity. This is the reason the automated market makers MSR, DPM, DPA and HSX have been developed. While it is obvious that a submitted order is not immediately executed in case of DAs, this is also the case for the HSX, as the execution occurs at the end of the sweep period. However, the number of traded shares is guaranteed with the HSX. With sufficient liquidity, all mechanisms except the CA and HSX are thus capable of instantly updating stock prices and thus pricing in new information. With the CA and HSX, however, price updates can only be accomplished at pre-determined points in time. Arbitrage possibilities by appropriately trading with AMMs are not given when using continuous price functions, which is the case of MSR and DPM. However, they do exist for DPA and HSX, and thus, have to be taken care of.

Regarding usability for traders, the DPM and the HSX stand out with two special properties. With the HSX, the final price of the share is determined at the end of the sweep period when all orders with corresponding quantities are available. Thus, this might be confusing for traders and could leverage uncertainty of trades. With the DPM, current stock prices in winner-takes-all markets do not directly reflect probabilities, but have to be transformed to probabilities. This poses an additional cognitive effort, which is likely to deter non-experienced traders.

From a PM operator's perspective, who has to implement and set up the market mechanisms for each market, the complexity of implementation plays a major role. In this case, DAs are advantageous, as there is no parameter value to choose which controls how the trading mechanisms behave. On the other hand, all AMMs have to be parameterized. MSR and DPM can be controlled with one single parameter, which controls the liquidity. The DPA needs three parameters to be set, while the HSX needs even more than three parameters. Another aspect concerns the use of real-money. If carefully set-up with unit-portfolios (2009b), DAs create no financial losses for the operator.

	Continuous double auction	Call auction	Market scoring rules	Dynamic pari-mutuel market	Dynamic price adjustment	HSX mechanism
General						
Unlimited buy-/sell liquidity	no	no	yes	yes	yes	yes
Immediate order execution	no	no	yes	yes	yes	no
Continuous price updates possible	yes	no	yes	yes	yes	no
Arbitrage free	n/a	n/a	yes	yes	no	no
Usability for traders						
Final price of shares known to user before trade	yes	yes	yes	yes	yes	no
Price of shares reflecting probabilities in case of 0/1 markets?	yes	yes	yes	no, to be transformed to probabilities	yes	yes
Operators perspective						
Number of parameters to set	0	0	1	1	3	> 3
Monetary losses	none, if unit-portfolios used	none, if unit-portfolios used	bounded	bounded	not bounded	not bounded

Table 2: Theoretical comparison of trading mechanisms (from Slamka et al. (2009b))

Simulative comparison of AMMs

Slamka et al. (2009b) compare all presented AMMs via an agent-based simulation of markets. The goal is to analyze forecasting accuracy, robustness of parameter selection and noisy trading, and the speed of information incorporation for each AMM, which are all important aspects when choosing an AMM besides theoretical considerations from above.

The simulation framework is split in three parts: the *market environment*, which assigns traders values such as valuations of stocks, the *market model*, which determines the interaction of traders with the AMM, and the *market result*, which captures the market outcome and the changes of predictions due to trading with the respective AMM. By keeping the market environment constant overall AMMs, it is possible to analyze the market result which is a consequence from the used AMM.

Traders most importantly receive signals about their valuation of the stock they trade and a constraint on the amount of money they can invest in shares or redeem by selling shares. The trader then tries to maximize his expected value from trading which results in the optimal number of shares he buys. The AMMs internal records are updated subsequently, and the forecasting accuracy, or deviation from the stock's underlying true value, can be measured.

In order to assess the forecast accuracy, the optimal parameters[7] for each AMM are determined with respect to the lowest overall absolute error. Overall, the DPM performs best, with a mean absolute error of 1.1 in 6000 replications (Table 3). The (logarithmic) MSR performs only slightly worse with an error of 1.25. The performance of the DPA is much worse and more than twice as bad as the one of the DPM with a mean absolute error of 2.25. However, HSX in its basic form performs worst with an error of 3.23.

[7] The HSX AMM is applied in a "basic" version with only three parameters, as the real mechanism is not fully documented.

	Logarithmic market scoring rules	Dynamic pari-mutuel market	Dynamic price adjustment	HSX mechanism
Mean MAE	1.254	1.101	2.253	3.233
Median MAE	1.083	0.989	1.203	2.137
Min. MAE	0.182	0.184	0.216	0.402
Max. MAE	5.380	4.024	10.949	15.955
Std. Dev. MAE	0.745	0.591	2.235	2.627
N	6000	6000	6000	6000

Table 3: Simulation results for overall forecasting accuracy (from Slamka et al. (2009b))

The knowledge about the consequences of misspecification of parameters is of importance when setting up markets and parameterizing the AMMs. The authors analyze deviations from the optimal parameter which controls the liquidity, i.e. how fast parameters move. As it can be seen from Table 12, when moving away from optimal parameters, the overall error hardly increases in case of DPM and LMSR, staying well under 30% increase. However, the error substantially increases in the case of the DPA, with far more than 100% if the deviation is -75% from the optimal parameter value. In this case, the performance of the HSX is better when compared with the DPA; however, it still shows more than an 80% error increase.

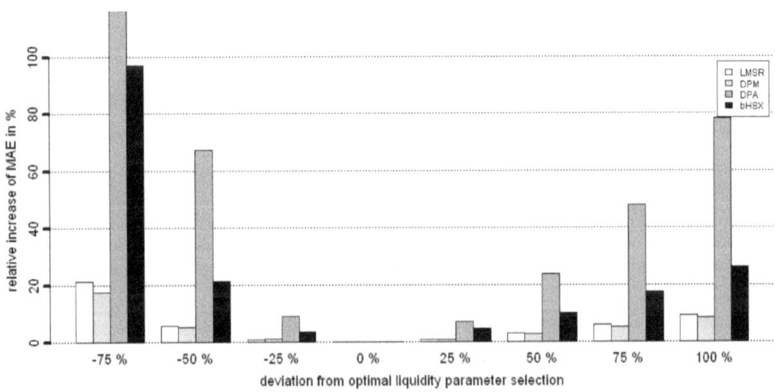

Figure 3: Deviations from optimal parameter selection and resulting increase of errors (from Slamka et al. (2009b))

When it comes to the influence of noisy trading behavior, i.e. not perfectly informed trading, on the market results, DPM as well as LMSR show to be very susceptible. I.e. the more traders have noisy information, in comparison to the perfectly informed traders, the worse the market results. Also, the worse a noisy trader is informed, the worse the market result is again. However, in contrast the HSX mechanism is not prone to noisy trading at all. If noisier trading occurs or noisy traders are informed worse, the market results do not significantly change. The DPA is slightly more susceptible to noisy trading, however, performing better than both DPM and LMSR.

When it comes to speed of information incorporation (Table 4), i.e. how fast new information is reflected in stock prices, we can see that LMSR and DPM are the fastest mechanisms, with a mean time of 9.79/8.13 periods to reach the new price level. On the other hand, the DPA is about twice as slow, needing more than 18 periods for information incorporation. The HSX is by far the slowest, with almost 30 periods needed.

	Logarithmic market scoring rules	**Dynamic pari-mutuel market**	**Dynamic price adjustment**	**HSX mechanism**
Mean no. periods	9.79	8.13	18.24	29.96
Median no. periods	4	7	18	30
Min. no. periods	0	0	0	0
Max. no. periods	106	37	98	140
Std. Dev. no. periods	17.29	6.86	12.74	22.67
N	2000	2000	2000	2000

Table 4: Speed of information incorporation (from Slamka et al. (2009b))

3.3. Incentives

Appropriate incentive schemes are required to motivate participation and to ensure information revelation in prediction markets. The traders' remuneration is crucial for the success of a market and consequently a key design element. Previous research in the field of prediction markets has shown that play-money as well as real-money markets can predict future events to a remarkable degree of accuracy. One relevant question is how much difference it actually makes whether markets are run with real money or with play money (Servan-Schreiber et al., 2004). Even though one might intuitively expect the performance of play-money markets to be worse than the performance of real-money markets, some have argued that "play money exchanges may even outperform real-money exchanges because 'wealth' can only be accumulated through a history of accurate predictions" (Chen and Plott, 2002, Ortner, 1997). A study of the predictions of the 2003 NFL football season has shown that the real-money market TradeSports and the play-money market NewsFutures predicted outcomes equally well (Wolfers and Zitzewitz, 2004).

Due to the legal restrictions on gambling many prediction markets are nowadays built up on play money. Some traders may be intrinsically motivated; but even in play-money markets the market operators can provide incentives such as a flat fee for participation or prizes for the largest play-money fortunes to remunerate traders. So far, market operators have employed various kinds of incentive schemes in order to motivate people to participate in such markets and to reveal their expectations. Typical incentive schemes include prizes for the top performers of a market, lotteries among all traders, rankings published on the World Wide Web. Based on earlier work by Luckner and Weinhardt (2007), we discuss selected incentive schemes for play-money markets and their impact on the accuracy of prediction in the following.

Three different monetary incentive schemes for play-money prediction markets are compared with regard to their impact on the accuracy of predictions. In order to do so, predictions from three groups of traders corresponding to three treatments with different incentive schemes are studied in a field experiment. Subjects of the first group received a fixed amount of money, subjects of the second group were paid according to their ordinal rank, and in the third group the subjects' payment depended linearly on their deposit value in the prediction market. Studying these incentive schemes is of special interest when traders need to be paid for taking part in a prediction market, e.g. in the case of an internal market for company-specific predictions. In such a market it is improbable that employees risk some of their own money in order to generate better company forecasts. Based on the results of the field experiment, advice on engineering incentive schemes for prediction markets is given.

3.3.1. Description of the Field Experiment on Monetary Incentives

The underlying events used for the field experiment were the outcomes of soccer matches. There were 20 markets for the last 20 matches of the FIFA World Cup 2006.

Contracts traded in the markets were the possible outcomes of all the matches. There were three possible outcomes for every match – either one of the two national soccer teams won or there was a draw after the second half, i.e. at the end of the regular playing time. The third contract "draw" was traded although there were no draws possible in 16 out of the 20 matches. The reason was that the outcome of overtimes and penalty shootouts was considered to be more or less unpredictable. The contract corresponding to the event that actually occurred during the World Cup was valued at 100 currency units after the match; the other two assets were worthless.

In total, 60 undergraduate students from the Universität Karlsruhe (TH), Germany, were taking part in the field experiment in June and July 2006. The operational principle of prediction markets was briefly explained in a lecture and students could then volunteer for the field experiment. After registering for the experiment they received subsequent instructions via e-mail. Moreover, the students were asked to complete a short pre-experiment questionnaire in order to collect demographic data and information about the students' risk attitude. All the markets opened two days before the corresponding match and closed at the end of the match. Traders were able to buy and sell basic portfolios comprising the three contracts traded in a market at 100 currency units at any time. This way, contracts were placed into circulation. The trading mechanism was a standard continuous double auction (CDA) with an open order book and limit orders. Short selling was not permitted.

The 60 students were randomly assigned to three groups of 20 students each. At the end of the FIFA World Cup 2006 the traders were paid in real money according to their group's incentive scheme. This allows for studying the impact of three different monetary incentive schemes by comparing the prediction accuracy of the three groups of traders, corresponding to three treatments with different incentive schemes. The subjects of the first group were paid a fixed amount of 50 Euro irrespective of how successful they traded in the markets (from now on referred to as fixed payment, FP). In the second group, individuals were paid according to their ordinal rank (rank-order tournament, RO). The trader ranked first within the group was paid 500 Euro, the second 300 Euro, and the third 200 Euro. All the other traders in this group did not receive any payment at all. Although the average payment is also 50 Euro per person, in this case, few traders win big prizes. Subjects in the third group were promised what was called a performance-compatible payment, also with an average amount of 50 Euro (deposit value, DV). Performance-compatible means that the payment linearly depended on the traders' success, i.e. the deposit value in the prediction market (deposit value divided by 10.000), and was therefore directly influenced by every transaction a trader carried out.

These three incentive schemes were chosen for the field experiment because they are closely related – although they admittedly are not exactly the same – to incentives that can nowadays typically be observed in public as well as corporate prediction markets. In case of public markets, there are usually markets without any payment or prizes to win, markets with rank-order tournaments, and real-money markets. Similarly, comparing the three monetary incentive schemes is also of interest for operators of internal markets for company-specific predictions. Companies are oftentimes willing to reward their employees' effort and so far used various incentives such as rankings demonstrating the expertise of successful traders, rank-order tournaments with big winners, and real-money markets where the employees' investments are subsidized by the company. These incentive schemes are again similar to the ones investigated in this field experiment and consequently the question arises which incentive scheme is the most suitable.

For every group, the 20 markets on 20 soccer matches of the FIFA World Cup were run separately, i.e. the same market existed three times. Aside from the difference in the incentive schemes, the market environment was identical across groups. This facilitates a more reliable test of the effect of incentives in prediction markets than has been reported in any of the related literature. Since subjects who did not trade at all should also not receive any payment, a relatively small minimum trading volume was imposed on all traders. The minimum weekly trading volume corresponded to 5 Euro in real money, i.e. 10 per cent of the initial deposit value. The weekly trading volume was displayed in the trading screen and subjects consequently always knew how much they had to trade in order to reach the minimum trading volume. Especially in the case of the fixed payment group subjects might otherwise have considered not trading at all or simply could have forgotten to participate in the online experiment.

3.3.2. Trading Activity

In general, the incentive scheme should influence the level of trading in a prediction market. In case of a fixed payment there is no monetary incentive to trade more than the minimum trading volume whereas a competitive incentive scheme such as the rank-order tournament should stimulate trading. Table 5 shows the total and mean number of trades as well as the standard deviation in the three treatments of the field experiment.

Treatment	# trades (total)	# trades (mean)	# trades (std dev)
FP (fixed payment)	1520	76	69.08
RO (rank-order tournament)	962	48.1	42.58
DV (deposit value)	1319	65.95	47.74

Table 5: Trading activity in the three treatments

Perhaps somewhat surprisingly, with a total of 1,520 the number of trades is highest in case of the treatment with the fixed payment and lowest in case of the rank-order tournament with a total of 962 trades. In the third treatment in which payments are linearly based on the traders' success, the number of trades lies between the other two treatments. Relative to the treatments with performance-based incentive schemes (RO and DV) the trading activity is higher than expected in the group with a fixed payment. The differences in trading activity between the three groups, however, are not statistically significant (Kruskal-Wallis test, p-value = 0.355)[8,9]. Despite the relatively high trading activity in case of the FP treatment, there was not a single trade in four markets. In the RO treatment, there were still two markets with no trading activity. This is of course undesirable because it is then impossible to derive any predictions from trading prices. The only treatment with trading activity in all markets was the DV treatment.

3.3.3. Trading Prices

In total, every group traded 60 contracts in 20 different markets. Figure 4 illustrates how many contracts were traded within certain price ranges in each of the three treatments. The prices under examination here are the last trading prices before the corresponding match started. Contracts are grouped into five price ranges and, for each treatment, the share of contracts with trading prices in each of the price ranges is depicted. The very

[8] The null hypothesis of the Kruskal-Wallis test states that there is no difference between the mean trading activities of the groups. The null hypothesis cannot be rejected here.

[9] Although the Kolmogorov-Smirnov test shows that distributions in each of the groups are normal, an analysis of variance cannot be used in this case because the variance of the data in the groups is not the same. The Bartlett's test was used to test for equal variances.

first column, for example, shows that before the match started 32% of the contracts were traded at prices between 0 and 20 virtual currency units in the first treatment with a fixed payment. Accordingly, in the RO treatment 19% of the contracts were traded within this price range.

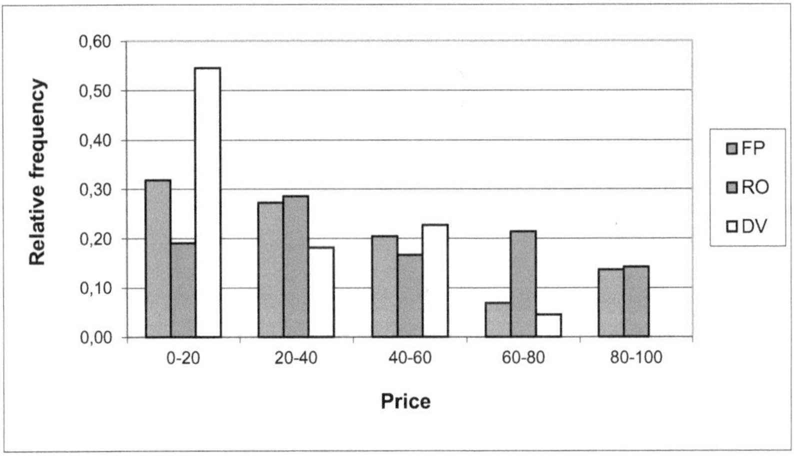

Figure 4: Distribution of trading prices in the three treatments FP (fixed payment), RO (rank-order tournament), DV (deposit value)

When comparing the three treatments one can see that a relatively high number of contracts were traded at prices between 60 and 100 currency units in the rank-order tournament treatment. Moreover, a relatively small number of contracts were traded at prices between 0 and 20 currency units in this treatment. Subjects are obviously willing to take some risk in treatment with the rank-order tournament and buy contracts even at rather high prices. In case the trading prices are good predictors the likelihood of the underlying events should be similarly high as the prices.

Subjects in the performance-compatible payment group, in contrast, do not trade any contract at a price between 80 and 100 currency units and almost no contract in the price range from 60 to 80. Obviously, traders with the payment scheme DV are unwilling to take the risk of buying contracts at such a high price although there is no reason why their expectations about specific outcomes of the matches should differ from the traders' expectations in the other two treatments. At the other extreme, 52% of the contracts are traded for less than 20 currency units in the DV treatment.

On average, trading prices for the same matches are lowest in the DV treatment and highest in the RO treatment. One possible explanation for the cautious behavior of traders in the third treatment could be their risk aversion. Due to their risk aversion, traders seem to trade contracts at lower prices compared to the other two treatments. Obviously, they are unwilling to buy contracts at prices similar to the ones in the other treatments and at the same time are willing to sell contracts at rather low prices. Traders in the RO treatment, however, are willing to take some risk in order to outperform the competing subjects of their group. The FP treatment does not impose any monetary risk at all and risk aversion thus should not matter. The following section discusses how this trading behavior impacts the prediction accuracy of the three treatments.

3.3.4. Predicting Accuracy

Overall, 35% of the contracts with the highest trading price out of the three contracts per match actually corresponded to the observed outcome in case of the fixed payment. This can also be referred to as hit rate of the markets. The average pre-game trading price of the contract corresponding to the outcome was 40.83 virtual currency units. In the rank-order tournament, the most likely outcome according to the trading prices actually occurred in 45% of the cases and the average pre-game trading price of the contract corresponding to the outcome was 51.65 currency units. Finally, in case of the performance-compatible payment, the most likely outcome according to the trading prices occurred in merely 20% of the cases and the average pre-game trading price of the contract corresponding to the outcome was 26.64 currency units. When interpreting the trading prices as probabilities the third group predicted the outcome of a match even worse than the treatment with a fixed payment. The rank-order tournament, in contrast, seems to work quite well with regard to the hit rate and average pre-game trading price. However, the differences between the average pre-game trading prices of the three treatments are not statistically significant (Kruskal-Wallis test, p-value = 0.156)[10]. Concerning the hit rate, there can only be found a statistically significant difference between the RO and the DV treatment (Pearson's chi-square test, p-value = 0.024)[11].

[10] The null hypothesis of the Kruskal-Wallis test cannot be rejected here and differences between the trading prices are thus not statistically significant.

[11] Although there was no trading activity in 4 markets in case of the FP treatment and in 2 markets in case of the RO treatment, the hit rate was calculated as the number of correctly predicted matches relative to the total number of matches. The hit rate of those two treatments would otherwise be a little higher. Nevertheless, this is not desirable since markets with no trades at all are also not useful for making predictions about the outcome of matches.

As was already described earlier, trading prices seemed to be rather low in case of the performance-compatible payment compared to the other treatments. This can also be seen when calculating the sum of the three contract prices corresponding to the three possible outcomes of a match. These prices should sum up to about 100 virtual currency units since the probability that one of the three events occurs is 100%. In case of the performance-related incentive scheme the average price of such a so called basic portfolio is only 53.30 virtual currency units while it is indeed very close to 100 in the other two treatments (97.72 in the FP treatment and 102.83 in the RO treatment). This is surprising because there is an arbitrage opportunity in case of such a deviation of the sum of the three contract prices from 100. Traders should buy all three contracts in a market and hold them or sell a basic portfolio since they get paid off on exactly one contract with certainty. But a thorough analysis of incoming and executed orders shows that it was impossible to buy all three contracts in a market at the same time for a sum of prices below 100 currency units. Traders as a consequence could not make use of arbitrage opportunities because the markets were not liquid enough. This also explains why the average pre-game trading price is extremely low in case of the DV group.

To analyze the correspondence between trading prices and outcome frequencies in more detail, the data was sorted into buckets by assigning all of the contracts to one of five price ranges according to their pre-game trading price.

Figure 5 plots the relative frequency of outcome against the trading prices observed before the corresponding match started.

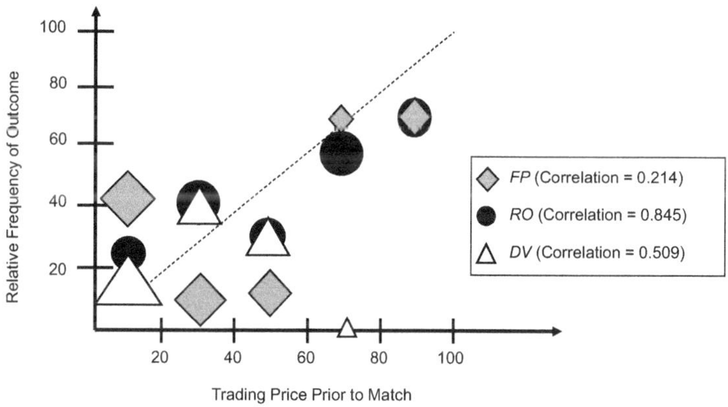

Figure 5: Market forecast probability and actual probability in the three treatments FP (fixed payment), RO (rank-order tournament), DV (deposit value)

If the markets are efficient, a plot of trading prices vs. observed outcome frequencies should approximate the 45-degree line which represents perfect accuracy. One should thus observe that contracts traded, for example, at a price of 30 currency units correspond to the actual outcome with a probability of 30% on average. The size of the circles, diamonds, and triangles indicates how many trading prices fall into the corresponding price range in case of the different incentive schemes. The larger a circle, diamonds, or triangle is, the more contracts were assigned to this price range.

A first glance at

Figure 5 already shows that the trading prices and outcome frequencies seem to correspond rather well in case of the rank-order tournament. The correlation between the relative frequency of outcome and the trading prices serves as an indicator for the accuracy of predictions[12]. For the rank-order tournament, the correlation coefficient is 0.845 which indicates a high correlation between outcome frequencies and trading prices. While there still is a medium correlation of 0.509 in case of the DV group, the correlation is not statistically significant for the predictions from the FP group[13]. Thus, trading prices from the RO group reach the highest correlation with outcome frequencies compared to the other two incentive schemes. Once again, the rank-order tournament seems to

[12] Spearman's rank correlation coefficient is employed to measure the correlation.
[13] p-value < 0.001 for RO and DV; p-value $= 0.082$ in case of FP

outperform the other incentive schemes. The prediction accuracy here is found to be better in case of the rank-order tournament than in case of the payment based linearly on the trading success in the DV treatment. The FP incentive scheme performs very poor as the correlation between trading prices and outcome frequency did not reach significance.

As was already discussed earlier, on average the sum of the three trading prices corresponding to the three possible outcomes of a match was only 53.30 virtual currency units in case of performance-compatible incentive scheme. Due to the low trading prices in the DV treatment there is no triangle in the price range between 80 and 100 currency units of

Figure 5. This lack might also explain why the prediction accuracy of the treatment with the rank-order tournament is higher. When dividing all the trading prices by the average price of a basic portfolio, in the DV treatment, the correlation coefficient between the relative frequency of outcome and the trading prices after all increases to 0.653[14]. Still, the correlation coefficient is higher in the RO treatment without any need for normalization. This result also makes the interpretation of trading prices as probabilities much easier in the RO treatment.

3.3.5. Discussion of Results

One can only speculate about possible reasons for this result, i.e. in particular the good performance of the rank-order tournament. Traders are obviously not only driven by monetary incentives since they do not stop trading as soon as they reach the minimum weekly trading volume in the FP treatment. Also, in case of the rank-order tournament, traders continue to trade even if winning becomes extremely unlikely for them. This explains why even the markets of the FP group work to some extent. Nevertheless, there was no trading activity for four matches and also no significant correlation between trading prices and outcome frequencies in case of the FP treatment. A fixed payment consequently does not seem to be a well-suited incentive scheme to remunerate traders in a play-money prediction market.

Still, intrinsic motivation does not explain the higher prediction accuracy of the RO treatment compared to the DV treatment since there is no obvious reason why intrinsic motivation should be different in these treatments. Both incentive schemes are performance-based but differ with respect to the accuracy of predictions. The traders'

[14] Spearman's rank correlation coefficient, p-value < 0.001

risk aversion could be one reason for the good performance of the rank-order tournament relative to the payment which depends linearly on the traders' success.

Before the field experiment on monetary incentives started, a lottery choice experiment as known from Holt and Laury (2002) was conducted in order to measure the traders' degree of risk aversion. Subjects were presented a menu of choices which permits measurement of the degree of risk aversion. The probabilities were explained in terms of throws of a ten-sided dice. The amounts of money were fifty times the ones used by Holt and Laury (2002). The choices thus involved large cash prizes that were paid to the subjects. The payoffs for Option A are less variable than the payoffs of the risky Option B. When the probability of the high-payoff outcome increases enough subjects should cross over from Option A to Option B. A risk-neutral subject would choose Option A four times before switching to Option B.

50 out of the 60 subjects from the field experiment also participated in the lottery choice experiment. Only 7 subjects ever switched back from B to A. Figure 6 depicts the average proportion of safe choices in the experiment as well as the risk neutral prediction for each of the ten decisions. One can see that the series of choice frequencies lies to the right of the risk neutral prediction. Across the three groups, nearly 75% of the subjects chose more than four safe choices and thus exhibited risk aversion. These results are in line with those reported in the literature (Holt and Laury, 2002, Harrison et al., 2007, Holt and Laury, 2005).

In case of the fixed payment, traders can neither win nor lose money, so they just play for fun and their risk aversion should not matter. Moreover, traders will take quite a lot of risk in the rank-order tournament because they have to be among the top performers within their group to receive the relatively large cash prize. Thus, the incentives over-ride risk aversion. Only in case of the performance-compatible incentive scheme, traders receive an endowment of 50 Euro and could potentially lose money with every trade they make. As a result, buyers are obviously extremely cautious and not willing to spend too much money on any contract. But why are sellers willing to give up contracts at prices below their average worth? Subjects had to trade in order to reach the minimum transaction volume. Once sellers have started to partially sell their basic portfolios they are probably willing to sell at rather low prices to avoid the risk of holding contracts of an event that does in the end not occur. Average trading prices are thus much lower than in case of the DV treatment than in the two other treatments. Evidently, the performance-compatible payment scheme is less suitable to reveal the traders' expectations about the likelihood of future events than the rank-order tournament.

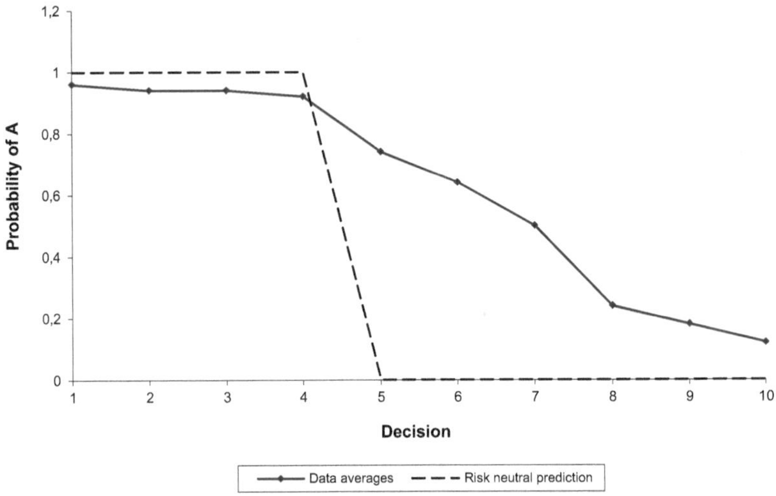

Figure 6: Proportion of safe choices in each decision

But what are the implications for designing incentive schemes of future prediction markets? Out of the three incentive schemes under examination in the field experiment prediction market operators should choose the rank-order tournament when, for example, setting up an internal market for company-specific predictions in which employees are to be rewarded for trading. Besides, performance-compatible payment schemes are somewhat similar to real-money markets. But is it now possible to draw the conclusion that play-money markets e.g. with prizes for the top performers will outperform real-money markets although the latter raise numerous legal and technical difficulties? One should rather be careful, when answering this question based on the results of the field experiment, because the situation might be somewhat different in prediction markets that are open to the public. In this case, there is a self-selection of traders and it is thus reasonable to expect that many traders in a public real-money market are risk-seeking. In such a situation a performance-compatible payment scheme might potentially produce much better predictions than in the case of the field experiment which is discussed here.

3.4. Traders

In the end, prediction markets only work, if traders with relevant information join the market and trade (Spann and Skiera, 2003). Market operators in consequence have to make sure they select traders with relevant information. One straightforward approach could be to invite experts who have access to information concerning the claims under study. This was usually done in corporate prediction markets, e.g. by Hewlett-Packard and Siemens (Wolfers and Zitzewitz, 2004). These markets had only between 20 and 60 traders and companies have repeatedly cited "motivating employees to participate" as an obstacle to a more wide-spread use of prediction markets (Forsythe et al., 1999). However, inviting experts only has at least two downsides.

Firstly, most prediction markets have very few participants compared to traditional financial markets. As a result, it is hard to fill an order book in a CDA market. The lack of offers to buy and sell limits the incentive for traders to reveal new information because they will have difficulty finding a trading partner for immediate trading. Replacing the widespread CDA by another trading mechanism is one approach to ensure that traders can profit from new information without having to find a trading partner. This downside can therefore be by-passed with a suitable market design.

Secondly and even more important, it is rather unlikely that there is a lot of disagreement among fully rational experts trading in a market. Disagreement about likely outcomes, however, is required to encourage trading (Hanson et al., 2006). Overconfident traders as well as an increase in noise trading should actually improve the accuracy of trading prices because this increases the rewards to informed trading – provided informed traders have deep pockets relative to the volume of noise trading. Instead of limiting the pool of traders to knowledgeable experts one should thus try to attract more traders. If traders self-select to join a market they usually have relevant information about and considerable interest in the claims under study. Nevertheless, one should avoid running markets on topics where insiders may possess substantially superior information or where information is concentrated on very few people. Such markets have historically attracted very little attention (2009a). Equilibrium prices may in this case not accurately reflect the true probabilities, because informed traders do not completely reveal their information. This can be explained by the fact that few informed traders can frequently benefit from fluctuating trading prices repeatedly and thus do not reveal their information at once.

Earlier research on prediction markets demonstrates that markets aggregate information and produce efficient outcomes despite biased individual traders (Wolfers and Zitzewitz, 2004). In the field of political stock markets, Forsythe et al. (1992) for the first time demonstrated that traders are buying and selling contracts of US presidential candidates in a manner which is correlated with their preferences, i.e. supporters of a candidate buy more contracts of this candidate than they sell. This is contradictory to the assumption that rational traders should not trade according to their individual preferences but according to the expected election outcome. Their preferences, however, seem to affect their expectations and traders might unconsciously support their preferred candidate or party. Forsythe et al. (1992) attribute the observed biases to failures in the traders' information-processing capabilities. However, manipulation should be considered as an alternative explanation for the traders' behavior in political stock markets. As a consequence, it appears reasonable to study the impact of traders' biases on their trading behavior in a field of application where traders cannot influence the outcome of the corresponding event.

Sports tournaments are supposed to be such a domain. In the following we thus give an example for biased trading from the sports prediction market STOCCER. We study the impact of the traders' nationality on their holdings and their trading behavior. If trading is correlated with preferences, traders should buy more and sell fewer contracts of their national team than other traders.

3.4.1. Field Study on Traders' Biases

We used data from the STOCCER FIFA World Cup market to study the correlation between the traders' nationality and their trading behavior. Contracts of all 32 national soccer teams were traded in this market. The contract of the world champion was redeemed at the highest value while contract of teams who had to quit the tournament after the preliminary round were worthless. Such a market is well suited to study the influence of the traders' nationality on their shareholdings and trading behavior since contracts of all national teams were traded in the market and the payoff of contracts depended on the overall performance of the teams. If biases related to the traders' country of origin existed, they should thus be observed in this market.

Every action of traders was recorded in the STOCCER championship market. Full information about the trading activity, i.e. orders and trades, and traders' shareholdings is available or can be calculated for any point in time. Moreover, the traders' nationality is known since they provided information about their country of origin during the registration process. Traders originated from 72 different countries around the world. Countries with a substantial number of traders were Germany, Switzerland, USA, Belgium, Austria, UK, China, and Italy. The number of traders from other countries is too small to allow for a meaningful analysis of traders' biases. Out of the eight aforementioned countries, the following analysis is restricted to countries which were taking part in the FIFA World Cup 2006. Hence, data on shareholdings as well as trading activity is analyzed to study biases of traders coming from Germany, Switzerland, USA, UK, and Italy. Traders in STOCCER are expected to be overly optimistic about their national team's likely success and to interpret news with respect to their national team more favorably than other traders. Thus, they should overestimate the likely success of their national team and make larger investments (number of contracts held) in their national team.

3.4.2. Traders' Nationality and Shareholdings

Similar to investors in financial markets who commonly allocate a large fraction of their portfolio to domestic investments, traders in the STOCCER championship market should hold more contracts of their country's national soccer team if they overestimate its likely success. Table 6 shows the average number of contracts held by traders originating from Germany, Switzerland, USA, UK, and Italy in the corresponding national teams at the market close on July 9th 2006[15]. Swiss traders, for instance, hold an average of about 1,153 contracts of the Swiss national team. They hold fewer contracts in the other four countries. On average across all 32 contracts traded in the market, Swiss traders hold only about 471 contracts.

		AVERAGE NUMBER OF CONTRACTS					
		Germany	Switzerland	USA	UK	Italy	Average
TRADERS' NATIONALITY	Germany	401.97	214.02	326.26	323.84	324.75	311.74
	Switzerland	189.39	1153.06	592.93	262.11	396.83	471.30
	USA	218.86	95.39	387.39	377.06	268.29	213.18
	UK	70.00	73.33	60.00	1347.60	543.87	446.30
	Italy	79.69	114.54	226.08	79.92	1406.54	277.71

Table 6: Traders' nationality and shareholdings in teams (July 9th 2006)

[15] The biases which are observed here are not specific for this point in time. We also looked at other points in time and the findings were very similar.

As a matter of fact, traders from all of these countries on average hold more shares in their own national team than in any of the other five teams. They also hold more contracts of their national team compared to the average team out of the 32 national soccer teams participating in the FIFA World Cup.

Figure 7 further highlights this bias by contrasting the average number of contracts held in the team of the traders' home country with the average number of contracts held across all teams on July 9th 2006. It can be seen that traders from Germany, Switzerland, USA, UK, and Italy indeed hold more contracts of their national team than of other teams. On average, the 1,306 traders coming from these five countries held about 546 contracts of their own national team compared to 336 contracts across all 32 teams[16]. The difference between the number of contracts held by traders in their national team and the number of contracts held across all teams is significant (Mann-Whitney U test, p-value < 0.001).

As a consequence, traders were biased in terms of holding more contracts of their own national soccer team than of other teams in the STOCCER championship markets. This can presumably be attributed to traders overestimating the likely success of their national team. If traders are more optimistic about their team than other traders, they should be willing to buy contracts at higher prices and thus also hold more contracts of their team than other traders.

[16] The standard deviation is 1503.72 for the contracts of the home country and 797.44 for all contracts.

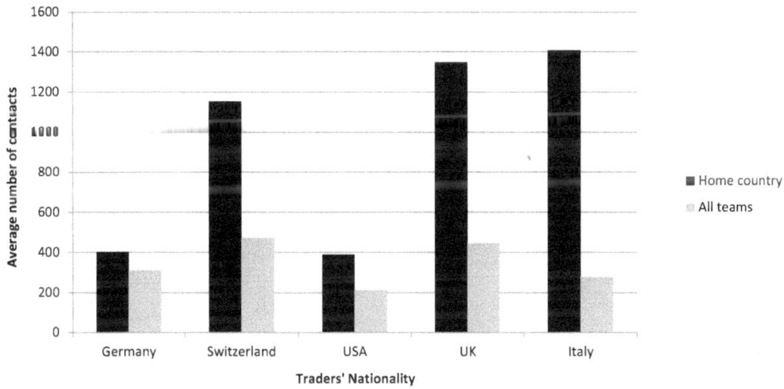

Figure 7: Shareholdings in home country and across all teams (July 9th 2006)

3.4.3. Traders' Nationality and Trading Behavior

Biases observed in the traders' shareholdings result from their trading behavior. This section therefore studies how biases resulting from the traders' nationality impact their trading behavior in the STOCCER championship market. Since traders hold more contracts of their own national team, there should be a larger proportion of net buyers among traders coming from the corresponding country compared to the proportion of net buyers among traders coming from other countries.

Table 7 shows the number and proportion of traders who purchased the contracts of the soccer teams from Germany, Switzerland, USA, UK, and Italy. For each contract, the traders are split up into two groups. The first group of traders comprises all traders coming from the country corresponding to the respective contract while the second group comprises all remaining traders. To give an example, there were 540 German traders who traded the contract "Germany". 413 out of these 540 traders bought at least one contract, i.e. the 127 remaining active traders only sold the contract. The proportion of German traders who bought the contract "Germany" thus is about 76 per cent whereas only about 57 per cent of non-German traders bought contracts of the German national team.

Contracts	Traders' nationality	# active traders	#traders who purchased	% of traders who purchased	p-value[17]
Germany	Germany	540	413	76.48%	<0.001
	Other	188	107	56.91%	
Switzerland	Switzerland	122	112	91.80%	<0.001
	Other	471	243	51.59%	
USA	USA	16	12	75.00%	0.006
	Other	591	245	41.46%	
UK	UK	9	6	66.67%	0.584
	Other	646	482	74.61%	
Italy	Italy	7	7	100.00%	0.102
	Other	619	448	72.37%	

Table 7: Traders' nationality and proportion of buyers

For four out of five contracts under investigation, the proportion of traders who purchased a contract was higher among traders coming from the corresponding country compared to the remaining traders. Merely in case of the UK, the proportion of traders who purchased is a little higher among non-UK traders than among UK traders. The difference in the proportion of traders is statistically significant for the contracts of Germany, Switzerland, and the United States of America (Pearson's chi-square test, see last column of Table 7). However, for the two contracts with a very small number of traders coming from the corresponding countries, i.e. UK and Italy, this difference is not statistically significant.

Table 8 follows the same idea but now shows the number and proportion of traders who sold the contracts of the five soccer teams. Again, the traders per contract are split up into the same two groups. For all five contracts, the proportion of traders who sold a contract was lower among traders coming from the corresponding country compared to the remaining traders. The difference in the proportion of traders is once more statistically significant for the contracts of Germany, Switzerland, and the United States of America (Pearson's chi-square test, see last column of Table 8). However, for the two contracts with a very small number of traders coming from the corresponding countries, i.e. UK and Italy, this difference is also not statistically significant.

[17] Chi-square test for difference in proportion of traders who purchased the corresponding contract

Contracts	Traders' nationality	# active traders	# traders who sold	% of traders who sold	p-value[18]
Germany	Germany	540	343	63.52%	0.001
	Other	188	132	70.21%	
Switzerland	Switzerland	122	58	47.54%	<0.001
	Other	471	385	81.74%	
USA	USA	16	8	50.00%	<0.001
	Other	591	530	89.68%	
UK	UK	9	4	44.44%	0.207
	Other	646	417	64.55%	
Italy	Italy	7	3	42.86%	0.170
	Other	619	416	67.21%	

Table 8: Traders' nationality and proportion of sellers

Overall, the traders' nationality seems to influence the proportion of traders who are buying and selling contracts. The proportion of traders buying a contract at all is larger among traders coming from the corresponding country compared to other traders and, vice versa, the proportion of traders selling a contract is lower among traders coming from the corresponding country compared to other traders.

Yet, the number of net buyers among the two groups of traders is even more worthy of note than the number of traders who are buying and selling contracts at all. Table 9 therefore compares the proportion of traders with net purchases among traders coming from the corresponding country to the proportion of traders with net purchases from other countries for each of the five contracts.

[18] Chi-square test for difference in proportion of traders who sold the corresponding contract

Contracts	Traders' nationality	# active traders	# traders with net purchases	% of traders with net purchases	p-value[19]
Germany	Germany	540	301	55.74%	<0.001
	Other	188	83	44.15%	
Switzerland	Switzerland	122	93	76.23%	<0.001
	Other	471	148	31.42%	
USA	USA	16	10	62.50%	<0.001
	Other	591	127	21.49%	
UK	UK	9	6	66.67%	0.345
	Other	646	329	50.93%	
Italy	Italy	7	5	71.43%	0.308
	Other	619	323	52.18%	

Table 9: Traders' nationality and proportion of traders with net purchases

As can be seen in Table 9, there is indeed a larger proportion of net buyers among traders coming from the corresponding country compared to the proportion of net buyers among traders coming from other countries for all the contracts under investigation. The difference in the proportion of traders with net purchases is once more statistically significant for the contracts of Germany, Switzerland, and the United States of America (Pearson's chi-square test, see last column of Table 9). For the two contracts UK and Italy with a very small number of traders coming from the corresponding countries the difference is again not statistically significant.

All in all, the traders' nationality influences their trading behavior. The differences in the proportion of net buyers can most likely be attributed to traders overestimating the likely success of their national team. They are more optimistic about their team than other traders and thus are more likely to become net buyers of contracts related to their national soccer team.

3.4.4. Discussion of Results

The results provide evidence that traders were biased in the STOCCER championship market. The traders' nationality influenced their trading behavior. Traders held more contracts of their own national soccer team than traders of a different nationality. Furthermore, the proportion of net buyers for all the contracts under investigation was found to be larger among traders coming from the corresponding country compared to the proportion of net buyers among traders coming from other countries.

[19] Chi-square test for difference in proportion of traders with net purchases

These results are in line with earlier findings in the field of political stock markets. Forsythe et al. (1992) found that traders are buying and selling contracts of US presidential candidates in a manner which is correlated with their preferences, i.e. supporters of a candidate buy more contracts of this candidate than they sell. Forsythe et al. (1992) attributed the observed biases to failures in the traders' information-processing capabilities. However, attempts of manipulation could also have explained the traders' behavior in political stock markets. The results reported here contribute to the literature by demonstrating that such biases can also be found in a field of application where traders are not likely to influence the outcome. In the case of STOCCER, traders are not likely to influence the outcome of soccer matches or the performance of their national soccer team. Thus, manipulation cannot serve as an explanation for the traders' behavior in the STOCCER championship market. Failures in the traders' information-processing capabilities for that reason can in fact be seen as a plausible explanation for the trading behavior which was found in STOCCER.

Interestingly, the predictions of the STOCCER championship market were found to be very accurate despite the biases which were found when looking at traders individually. Presumably, biases of a group of traders such as the traders coming from a certain country can be compensated by the remaining traders as long as the proportion of traders with biases in favor of the same contract is not too large. Similar to this, Hanson et al. (2006) found that subjects in an experimental market compensated for the bias in offers from manipulators who were submitting higher price offers by setting a different threshold at which they were willing to accept trades. As a result, the distortionary effects of manipulation were cancelled out in the experiment.

This also has important implications for selecting traders of prediction markets. Traders' biases most likely do not distort prediction accuracy if other traders are compensating for these biases. Prediction market operators thus have to ensure that not all traders exhibit the same bias. Otherwise, traders' biases could indeed distort trading prices and thereby also the prediction accuracy.

3.5. Trading Software

Designing a prediction market system not only affords the abstract market system behind the scenes to work properly as seen in the preceding sections, but also the implemented market system to satisfy certain needs. As an information service a prediction market system can be characterized by three major abstract components, namely the user interface as the connection to the user, the software that provides the user interface and the market functionality, and the hardware infrastructure on top of which the whole system works.

3.5.1. User Interface

Depending on the target audience the user interface of a prediction market system is depending on a good and attractive design. First of all this is depending on the users' home country (languages), technical and cultural background (metaphors with different meanings), colors (i.e. white as mourning color in Japan), and meanings of words. But also the target audience and their incentivation are key to a successful design. For example, working in the area of a research experiment with the traders paid for their participation: These users have a quite different incentive to the users within a public prediction market system, where the users' technical background can be problematic and the system layout has to compete with other online content. Moreover within the public system the users have to be incentivized by the system itself rather than by extrinsic means (payment for participation). This is even more important in the area of web 2.0 where online content has to meet the standards of the community the site is built for (i.e. additional software like community function etc.). The topics discussed in Table 10 give an overview on the user interface design aspects.

Topic	**Determinants**	**Range**
Internationalization	country of the user, audience addressed	single language (English) -> multilingual frontend
Browser compatibility	users' operating system, browser family, browser version, plugins	based on most common browser -> multibrowser capable
Types of user interface	users' technical background of audience addressed	Common internet site -> user-oriented interfaces (i.e. broker screen)
Complexity of the topic, Metaphor	users' educational background, state of knowledge (newspaper-reader, broker)	diversification of functionality (novice vs. pro functionality), FAQ
Unknown topic	users' educational background, state of knowledge (newspaper-reader, broker)	differentiation in metaphor (other than stock-market paradigm)

Table 10: Important user interface design aspects for a prediction market system

3.5.2. Software Specification

As prediction markets usually are based on a programmed infrastructure, certain aspects of software development are crucial to the design of a proper prediction market system. In the row of these aspects *scalability* of the programmed infrastructure is key for an environment aiming at economic operation. If the software is designed to conduct solely expert markets with a small number of traders, scalability is indeed insignificant. But as in modern programming languages at least the kernel of such software is usually reused in other projects, it is to be advised to keep this aspect prioritized. Thereby scalability denotes the performance in dealing with a multitude of actors (traders) or a multitude of actions by the existing actors (trades). Both should be thoroughly accounted for in all parts of the programming work.

Often depending on the scalability, the *response-times* and the *service of serving* the content by the server providing the prediction market should be stable. As a prediction markets' legitimation is directly dependent on the integrity of its service, the security of the software is key for a valid prediction market system itself. This security does not only include the encryption layer between the user and the system, but especially the setup of an incentive compatible system-status and a working fraud detection for absorbing incentive incompatibilities (see Schröder (2009)).

Within the software a prediction market's user interface consists of the following functional elements: screen for trading shares, screen for trading portfolios, order books of the shares, information on the share (price plots, more information), information on the market (price plots, more information), ranking, illustration of the incentive system, terms, help-system.

3.5.3. Hardware Specification

The requirements of the technical infrastructure are basically driven by the surrounding the prediction market system is set up in. As in the software specification, the knowledge about the locale of origin of the traders is crucial. A prediction market is an online stock-trading system and as such subject to a real-time operation that asks for high availability of the service, especially on the network layers. But also with the scalability of the amount of users the hardware has to deliver a proper software service and is therefore strongly interconnected to the scalability of the software, especially the database layer. Given a service that provides a continuous operation in all stages in regard to scaling, the service then has to provide hardware integrity. To provide a proper hardware safety especially for a prediction market system the essential design aspects are: Application of adequate firewall solutions, backup systems, access control to the servers, fire protection, external safety monitoring (regular profession and comprehensible examination on weak points within the hardware infrastructure), redundant hard disk systems, availability of replacement systems, intrusion detection systems for determining and pursuing cybercrime. The flexibility of the implementation is depending on the operational area and the uncertainty concerning the number of participants. Depending on the desired application the system is implemented as a static single application on a central server, or a distributed concept deployable in various environments.

3.5.4. General Requirements

As overall aspects of the discussed system, data security is a strong issue on both, the hardware and the software side. This is dependent on the jurisdiction of the areas the software is provided in. In general this aspect asks for the separation of the participants' personal data (address, personal info) and the system data (trading data). Also a certain level of anonymization is to be provided in the cases of exporting data. In many countries (e.g. Germany) an agreement with each user about the handling of the personal data is demanded and has to take place before any action within the system. To provide a sustainable and enduring software system the overall design should allow for a flexible layout engine, the integration of multimedia elements, templating, and widgeting.

4. Applications of Prediction Markets

This chapter presents previous fields of application of prediction markets. Subsequently, we discuss several field experiments in more detail. We start with a description of the 2006 FIFA World Cup prediction market called STOCCER. Moreover, we also present the political stock market PSM and the Australian Knowledge eXchange AKX. At the end of the chapter we give an outlook on how prediction markets can be used to generate and evaluate innovative products and services.

4.1. Previous Fields of Application

Prediction markets have already been applied successfully in various domains. We believe it is important to differentiate between short and medium term forecasts on the one hand and on long term forecasts or evaluations of concepts on the other hand. So far, prediction markets were mostly used for short and medium term forecasts. We will give a number of examples for such markets in the following section. However, they also have a huge potential in long term forecasting and the evaluation of concepts, although designing such markets is rather challenging, e.g. with regard to determining the final value of the contracts which are traded in the market.

4.1.1. Short and Medium Term Forecasts

This section gives an overview of previous fields of application of prediction markets for short and medium term forecasts that have been reported in the literature. Since it is all but impossible to consider the totality of earlier applications, the list of applications given in Table 11 was compiled based on an extended literature review which was published in the Journal of Prediction Markets in an attempt to collect the totality of academic work related to short and medium term forecasting with prediction markets (Tziralis and Tatsiopoulos, 2007a).

Field of Application	Name of Market	Focus	Reference
Political stock markets	Iowa Electronic Markets	US presidential elections, non-US elections (e.g. Austria, France,	Berg et al. (2001), Berg et al. (1996), Berg et al. (1997), Berg and Rietz (2003), Berg et al. Berg and

Field of Application	Name of Market	Focus	Reference
		Korea, Germany)	Rietz (2006), Bondarenko and Bossaerts (2000), Erikson and Wlezien (2006), Forsythe et al. (1994), Forsythe et al. (1992), Forsythe et al. (1999), Fowler (2006), Kou and Sobel (2004), Oliven and Rietz (2004)
	UBC election stock market	Provincial and federal elections in Canada	Antweiler and Ross (1998), Forsythe et al. (1995), Forsythe et al. (1998)
	Swedish EU PSM	Swedish 1994 EU referendum	Bohm and Sonnegard (1999)
	GEM 90, GEM 91, GEM 94, GEM 98	Federal and regional elections in Germany	Brüggelambert (2004)
	Wahlstreet, Wahlboerse	State elections in Germany	Hansen et al. (2004)
	Passauer Wahlbörse	Federal elections in Germany	Beckmann and Werding (1996)
	The Political Stock Market	Federal and provincial elections in Germany	Franke et al. (2006), Franke et al. (2005)
	NP02, TE03	National assembly and regional elections in Austria	Huber and Hauser (2005)

Field of Application	Name of Market	Focus	Reference
	"Die Presse" Election Market	Elections for the national assembly in Austria 2002	Filzmaier et al. (2003)
	Austrian Political Stock Market	Austria's membership in the EU, federal elections, governing coalition	Ortner et al. (1995)
	PAM94	European Parliament and municipal councils in the Netherlands	Jacobsen et al. (2000)
Sports prediction markets	TradeSports	Worldwide sports prediction market, e.g. baseball, soccer, football	Chen et al. (2005), Rosenbloom and Notz (2006), Servan-Schreiber et al. (2004)
	NewsFutures	Sports (e.g. baseball, football, soccer), political elections	Chen et al. (2005) , Rosenbloom and Notz (2006), Servan-Schreiber et al. (2004)
	World Sports Exchange	Football, baseball, hockey, basketball etc.	Debnath et al. (2003)
	Betfair	Soccer, tennis, horse racing, etc.	Smith et al. (2006)
	Bundesligabörse	Soccer	Spann and Skiera (2009)
Other	Hollywood Stock	Box office performance of	Gruca et al. (2003), Pennock et al. (2001b), Pennock et al.

Field of Application	Name of Market	Focus	Reference
applications	Exchange	movies	Pennock et al. (2001a), Spann and Skiera (2003), Foutz and Jank (2010)
	CMXX	Success of movies, music CD's and video games in Germany	Skiera and Spann (2004)
	Economic Derivatives	Retail sales, GDP, international trade balance, growth in payrolls	Gürkaynak and Wolfers (2006)
	Idea Markets	Prediction of Success of New Product Ideas	Soukhoroukova et al. (2010)

Table 11: Fields of application of prediction markets

Table 11 comprises all applications of short and medium term forecasting which were reported in journal articles, books or book chapters, and conference proceedings papers referenced in the aforementioned literature review. Pure lab experiments where signals are e.g. drawn from an urn were not taken into consideration. The applications were grouped into three categories: political stock markets, sports prediction markets, and other applications. Due to the fact that most of the longest running prediction markets were originally set up to forecast political elections or the outcome of sports tournaments, academic research has largely concentrated on political stock markets and sports prediction markets. The following subsections provide some more information on the three categories of applications.

Political Stock Markets

Beside early introductory articles by Hanson (Hanson, 1990a, Hanson, 1990b, Hanson, 1992), most of the literature on prediction markets up until 1998 is on political stock markets. The most cited and earliest application of a political stock market on the internet, the Iowa Electronic Markets (IEM[20]), was established in 1988 by the University of Iowa. The IEM were designed to give students a hands-on experience in trading and to study market dynamics. The first academic article on the IEM was published in 1992 (Forsythe et al., 1992). IEM focussed on US presidential and state elections, but the platform was also used to run political stock markets on elections e.g. in Austria, France, Korea, and Germany. Predictions derived from IEM trading prices have been more accurate than their natural benchmark, namely polls, although traders exhibit biases (Berg et al., 2001, Forsythe et al., 1999). Moreover, trading prices react extremely quickly to new information (Berg and Rietz, 2006). In the meanwhile the IEM are not only used for predicting the outcome of political elections but also in order to predict e.g. economic indicators. Beside predicting uncertain future events the IEM were also studied as a decision support system where decisions are made based on trading prices (Berg and Rietz, 2003).

Other political stock markets in Canada (e.g. Antweiler and Ross, 1998), Sweden (Bohm and Sonnegard, 1999), Germany (e.g. Beckmann and Werding, 1996), and Austria (e.g. Ortner et al., 1995) have been set up with a similar research focus. Furthermore, these markets were also used to study manipulation in prediction markets (Hansen et al., 2004). All in all, political stock markets have in many cases outperformed traditional polls (Berg et al., 2001). Due to this reason they have received quite a lot of attention in the media and several publishing houses have already been running their own markets (Filzmaier et al., 2003).

Sports Prediction Markets

Sports prediction markets like Betfair.com[21], the World Sports Exchange[22], and TradeSports[23] are among the most popular prediction markets. These markets focus on forecasting the outcome of sports tournaments and events. Among popular sports are e.g. baseball, soccer, football, hockey, basketball, tennis, and horse racing. Earlier studies on sports prediction markets show that these markets provide at least as accurate predictions as experts (Chen et al., 2005, Servan-Schreiber et al., 2004) or better (Spann and Skiera, 2009). In accordance with the efficient market hypothesis game events are quickly

[20] http://www.biz.uiowa.edu/iem/
[21] http://www.betfair.com
[22] http://de.wsex.com
[23] http://www.tradesports.com

resulting in changes of trading prices. Smith et al. (2006) find that markets on UK horse racing exhibit both weak and strong form of market efficiency.

One precondition for exploiting the potential of prediction markets is to provide incentives for participation and information revelation. Therefore, prediction markets such as the IEM require real-money investment from traders. In case of the IEM these investments are limited to a maximum amount of US$ 500. As was already mentioned in Section 3.3 two articles in the field of sports prediction markets, however, show that there is no significant difference in terms of prediction accuracy between play-money and real-money prediction markets (Rosenbloom and Notz, 2006, Servan-Schreiber et al., 2004).

Other Applications

Nowadays, prediction markets are increasingly employed in innovative fields of application beyond political stock markets and sports prediction markets. One popular example is the Hollywood Stock Exchange (HSX[24]), a prediction market where traders forecast box office revenues of films, both for opening weekends and beyond. CMXX.com was a similar market operated in Germany to predict the success of movies, music CD's, and video games (Skiera and Spann, 2004). Pennock et al. (2001a) demonstrated that trading prices in the HSX movie markets are good predictors of the box office performance of movies. Based on these forecasts the movie industry can then make decisions on how to allocate advertising based on expected box office revenues. This shows how companies can use prediction markets to make better informed decisions.

Apart from predicting box office revenues, markets can be used broadly for predicting the success of all kinds of new products (Gruca et al., 2003). Successful examples for such markets are the simExchange[25], a market for predicting the sales of console hardware and upcoming video games, an internal market run by Eli Lilly to find out which drugs will be most successful (Kiviat, 2004) or the idea market conducted by Soukhoroukova (2011) in a large, high-tech B2B company with more than 500 participants from 17 countries. Another interesting field of application is the prediction of macroeconomic data such as retail sales, GDP, international trade balance, and the

[24] http://www.hsx.com
[25] http://www.thesimexchange.com

growth in payrolls. For this purpose a market called "Economic Derivatives" was launched in 2002. A first analysis shows that the expectations reflected in trading prices are similar to survey-based predictions (Gürkaynak and Wolfers, 2006).

Other prominent examples of companies using prediction markets internally are Hewlett-Packard, where traders produced more accurate forecasts of printer sales than the company's forecasting team (Chen and Plott, 2002) or Siemens, where software developers predicted the completion date of a huge software project (Ortner, 1997).

4.1.2. Long Term Forecasts and Evaluation of Concepts

Potential areas of application

In the previous studies, many interesting and valuable applications of PMs for managerially important questions were exhibited. However, traditional PMs as applied in these studies suffer from one important shortcoming: the outcome of an event must be known in the short- or medium-term in order to determine the stocks' payoffs and to incentivize participants to trade and to reveal their beliefs. Today six studies (see Figure 8) consider forecasting of non-actual events, i.e. events whose payoffs can either very late or (partially) never be determined, however, their results promise further areas for future research and extended application of PMs. The approach, how these studies deal with the problem of non-existing payoffs, is further discussed below.

One part of applications with non-actual events is concerned with cases where the outcome will be known, but only in the far future (see Figure 8). I.e., at that point in time, e.g. some years from now, the market might not be running any more or participants might have changed due to rotations in company's staff. Thus, clearing the market by paying off the stocks becomes unfeasible for this kind of questions. However, with the great success of PMs in aggregating asymmetric information, long-term questions such as corporate strategic questions or forecasting of future technologies are important in the managerial context.

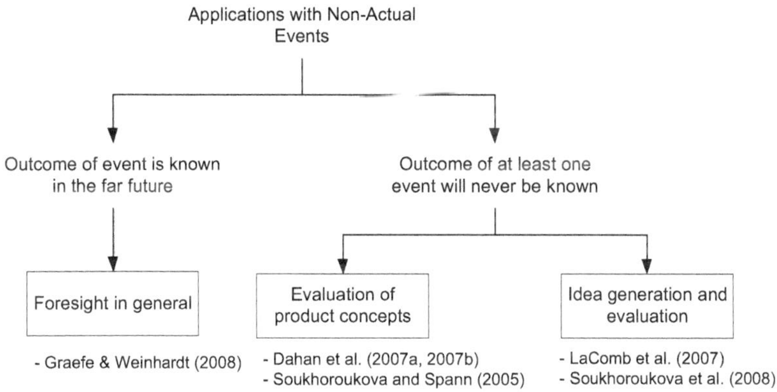

Figure 8: Classification of applications with non-actual events (from Slamka et al. (2009a))

The other part of potential applications concerns those where at least one outcome of an event in a market will definitely not be known. This happens when PMs are used to make choices between alternatives, such as among future products, and only a subset of all possible alternatives is chosen to be implemented in reality. Now clearly, if the chosen alternative is implemented and its success can be measured within an acceptable time frame, the payoff for this alternative can be determined. However, this is not the case for the remaining alternatives which were not chosen to be implemented. Consequently, a payoff cannot be observed. Typical cases in corporate settings, especially in the new product development process, involve the evaluation of product concepts, where from a large number of alternatives, only few make it to the market. Extension of this evaluations have been already been applied in so-called idea-markets, where participants not only evaluate product ideas, but also suggest them.

Description of studies

Six studies as we are aware of today, deal with the problem of forecasting non-actual events with payoffs either determined market-internally or –externally. Four studies use internal measures. LaComb et al. (2007) study an "imagination market", where company-internal participants generate and evaluate business and product ideas. The final payoff was based on the volume-weighted average price (vwap) over the last 5 trading days prior to the close of the market. On the other hand, using the last traded price as payoff, the studies of Chan et al. (2007) and Soukhoroukova and Spann (2005) test new products. Dahan et al. (2009) also use the last traded price (last-price) as payoff, however, in contrast to the former studies, they close the market at a random point in time (last-price-random-close) to avoid last minute market movements. Two recent studies use external proxy measures to determine payoff. In a study comparable to the "imagination market" (Graefe and Weinhardt, 2008), Soukhoroukova et al. (2009) create an "idea market" to generate new product ideas for a high-tech company. In contrast to aforementioned studies, they base the payoffs on the assessment of a corporate-internal expert committee, and thus a market-external source. Graefe & Weinhardt (2002), in a field experiment, use a Delphi study with external experts which did not participate in the markets, to determine the payoffs in markets involving a group of students and a group of experts.

Study	Application	Payoff of stocks based on (internal or external measure)	(Theoretical) comparison to alternative instruments
LaComb et al. (2005, 2007)	"Imagination market", creating and evaluating ideas	Volume-weighted average trading price over last trading days	-More ideas and more participants compared to traditional methods
		(market-internal)	- immediate feedback, visibility of ideas, fun mechanism
Chan et al. (2007)	Consumer preferences of new product concepts	Last trading price before close of market	- Cheaper, less time-consuming and less biased compared to e.g. surveys, conjoint studies, focus groups or concept tests
		(market-internal)	
Soukhoroukova and Spann (2005)	Consumer preferences of new product concepts	Last trading price before close of market	- Cheaper, need for less subjects than conjoint study
		(market-internal)	
Dahan et al. (2009)	Consumer preferences of new product concepts with high number of product features	Last trading price before random close of market	- High scalability with respect to number of features
		(market-internal)	- engaging and fun task
			- but: no individual preferences
Soukhoroukova et al. (2009)	Creating and evaluating new products with a company-internal	Expert committee	- Only method which involves large number of ideas and creators, group decisions and combination of idea creation and combination
		(market-external)	
Graefe & Weinhardt (2008)	Long-term forecasting of future trends	Delphi study	- Delphi study
		(market-external)	

Table 12: Studies of prediction markets with non-actual outcomes

The problem of determining payoffs

The main problem with all of these studies is, in contrast to "traditional" PMs, that if a stock's payoff cannot be determined, the subsequent evaluation of traders according to their performance remains impossible. However, for many managerially relevant questions, "true values" of events might not be available within an acceptable time frame or might never be known at all.

Thus, the key challenge when dealing with non-actual events is to replace the payoff function in actual outcome markets with an alternative payoff which determines the final rankings of traders. This alternative payoff is then independent of any "true" state of the underlying event to be forecasted and consequently, must be constructed otherwise.

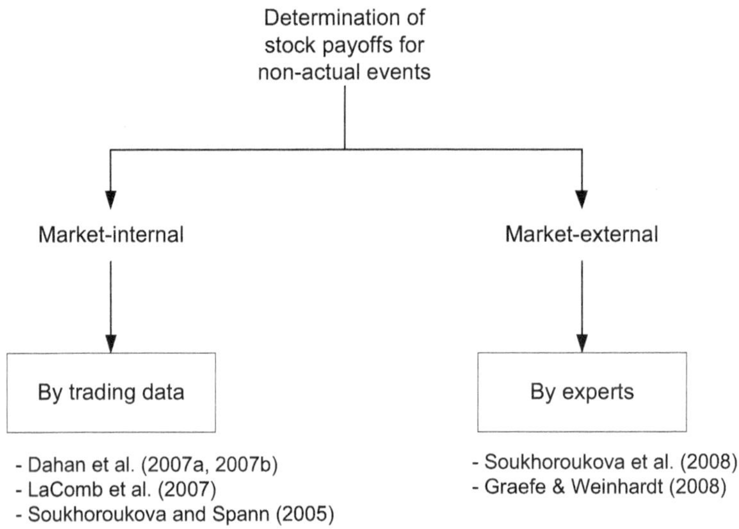

Figure 9: Alternative general approaches to determine payoffs (from Slamka et al. (2009a))

In general, the literature has proposed two general possibilities to determine the payoff of a stock. First, payoffs can be determined market-internally by only using data from the trading activity (cf. Figure 9). In this case, the trading actions as such serve as proxy for the payoffs. Second, payoffs can be determined market-externally by a proxy measure which is independent of the trading data in the particular market. Here, experts could be questioned on their assessments, and their aggregated assessments could be used as payoffs. However, using market-external payoffs by experts exhibits some disadvantages. The costs are higher to acquire experts, if they are available at all. Then, again, expert opinions have to be aggregated again. Last, traders might predict potentially biased expert decisions, rather than inputting their own assessments.

Evaluation of alternative payoffs

Despite the different suggestions how to determine payoffs in non-actual markets, statements about their external validity were not present. Therefore, Slamka et al. (2008) carry out a theoretical analysis of market-internal payoffs (volume-weighted average price, last price and last price random close) and conduct an experiment in order to determine the external validity and analyze trading behavior. The crucial element of the experiment is that it is based on events which actually occur – thus, external validity can be tested by comparing the results of the alternative market to a "traditional" prediction market, which is run in parallel. The only difference is that the payoffs alternative payoff markets are based on the respective payoff mechanism, while the traditional prediction markets' payoff is based on the outcome of the event.

The experiment consists of three runs of consecutive markets with MBA students and three different topics, that is to say politics, sports and economy. With three topics, four different payoffs including the "traditional" payoff, two replications for each payoff and ten stocks on average per market, a total of 240 shares can be analyzed.

	Actual outcome with students	Vwap (volume-weighted average price)	Last-price	Last-price-random-close
Topic 1 (Politics)				
Mean abs. error	18.15	30.70	23.39	31.66
Std. error	3.62	5.03	4.21	5.10
N	22	22	22	22
Topic 2 (Sports)				
Mean abs. error	31.22	27.77	30.49	29.30
Std. error	6.50	6.31	6.66	5.71
N	20	20	20	20
Topic 3 (Economy)				
Mean abs. error	39.28	46.05	48.37	41.83
Std. error	6.34	6.93	5.85	5.70
N	18	18	18	18
All				
Mean abs. error	28.85	34.33	33.25	33.92
Std. error	3.37	3.63	3.49	3.24
N	60	60	60	60

Table 13: Mean absolute errors across experiments (from Slamka et al. (2009a))

As it can be inferred from Table 13, the mean absolute error is on average slightly higher for alternative payoffs (28.85 vs. 34.33/33.25/33.92), which was to be expected. However, the difference of 4.4 points of actual markets to last-price markets is only marginal. The other two payoffs perform comparable. However, it is surprising that the relative forecast accuracy of actual and alternative payoffs varies between different topics. While the actual markets have been clearly superior in the topics of politics and economy, they even perform slightly worse in sports.

The good results of alternative payoff markets are surprising in the sense that in theory and observed as in practice in the experiments, they exhibit certain disadvantages. This includes herding behavior, last minute trading, or excessive trading during regular trading hours. We can thus say that markets based on alternative, market-internal payoffs are valid for information aggregation with high external validity. In consequence, markets dealing with non-actual events such as preference markets, idea markets or long-term forecasting markets are plausible new application areas of the traditional prediction market concept.

4.2. Results from Selected Field Experiments

This section gives an overview over three field experiments, their setup and results. We start with the STOCCER platform that was used to investigate the prediction accuracy of markets with respect to sports events in an international context and show results concerning the performance in comparison to other predictions. In section 4.2.2, the Political Stock Market PSM is introduced as a platform focusing mainly on election prediction, and results from three different markets are used to illustrate key aspects of market operation. Finally, section 4.2.3 describes the Australian Knowledge Exchange AKX that was used to predict the water levels in several Australian reservoirs using an expert market.

4.2.1. STOCCER – A Sports Prediction Market

This section describes a 2006 FIFA World Cup prediction market called STOCCER. Most of the data which is used to answer the research questions in the following three chapters comes from the STOCCER prediction market. Section 4.2.1.1 describes the FIFA World Cup 2006 itself before Section 4.2.1.2 presents the STOCCER exchange including its key design elements as well as information about traders and the trading activity.

4.2.1.1. The FIFA World Cup 2006

The most important soccer tournament worldwide in 2006, the FIFA World Cup, was held in Germany from June 9th to July 9th 2006 with 32 participating national teams which had qualified for the tournament. The tournament was organized in two stages – a group stage and a knock-out stage. All in all, 48 matches were played in the group stage and 16 in the knock-out stage, resulting in a total of 64 matches.

In the group stage the teams played round robin in eight groups of four to qualify for the knock-out stage. The winning team of a match received three points, the losing team received zero points, and in case of a draw after 90 minutes each team received one point. The two most successful teams in each group advanced to the knock-out stage. If two or more teams achieved the same number of points the direct comparison, i.e. the results of the match(es) against each other, was used as a tie-breaker. Further subordinate tie-breakers are the difference between the numbers of goals scored and received, the total number of goals scored in the group stage, the FIFA country coefficient from the FIFA world ranking, and finally tossing a coin.

In the knock-out stage, which started on June 24, the winning team of a group played the second of one of the remaining groups. All the matches in the knock-out stage were played in a sudden death system. Additionally, one game was played for the third place between the losers of the two semi-final games. In case of a draw after regular time in the knock-out stage the match was continued for an extra time of two times fifteen minutes. If a match was still not decided after extra time, there were penalty shootouts. The winner of a match in the knock-out stage advanced to the next round. Figure 10 shows all the 16 matches from the knock-out stage of the FIFA World Cup 2006.

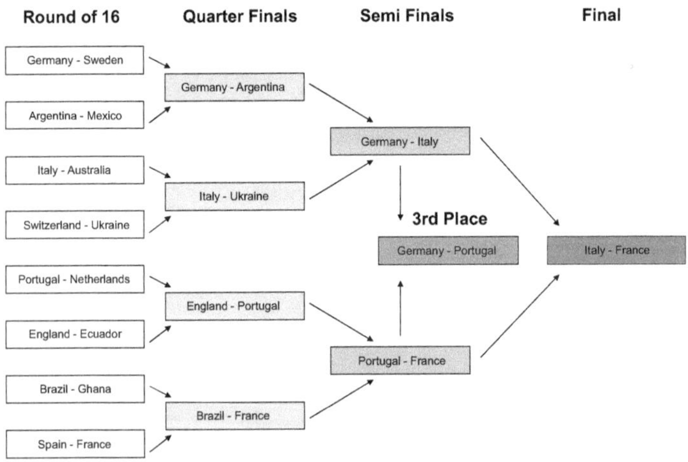

Figure 10: Knock-out stage of the FIFA World Cup 2006

The tournament was won by Italy, defeating France in a penalty shootout after extra time finished in a draw. Germany defeated Portugal to finish third. After the sometimes surprising 2002 tournament, the FIFA World Cup 2006 was dominated by traditional soccer powers. Six former champions took part in the quarter-finals with Ukraine and Portugal remaining as the only relative outsiders.

4.2.1.2. The STOCCER Exchange

STOCCER was operated before and during the 2006 FIFA World Cup in order to predict the outcome of the tournament, the outcome of particularly exiting matches, and the tournament's top goal scorer. In total, more than 1.700 traders registered with the play-money prediction market STOCCER[26]. The first market started on May 15th 2006 and ran until the end of the FIFA World Cup on July 9th 2006. The trading platform was open to the public 24 hours a day, 7 days a week. On average, there were more than 1,600 trades per day with a total number of about 90,000 trades. The continuous increase in the number of registered users as well as the development of the trading activity through time is illustrated in Figure 11. The upsurge in the number of users and the number of trades per day around June 9th 2006 can without much doubt be explained as follows. First of all, the opening match took place that day and consequently there was a lot of interest in the tournament. Furthermore, several newspaper articles on the STOCCER exchange were published at that time and the markets were thus made known to a larger audience.

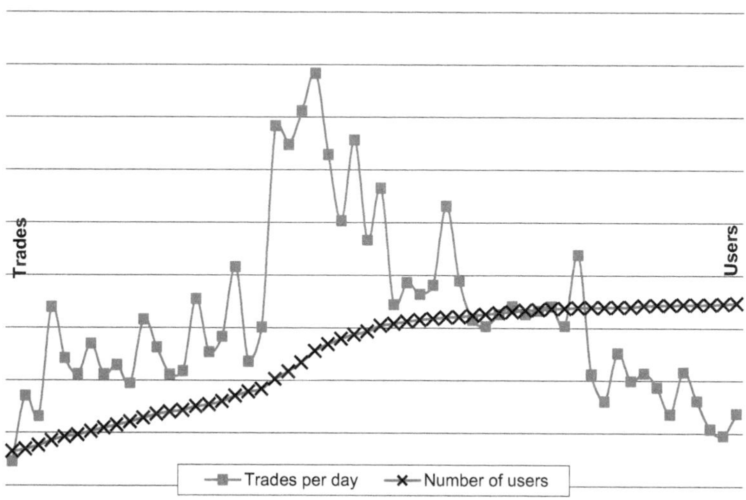

Figure 11: Number of users and trading activity over time

[26] http://www.stoccer.com. The STOCCER project was funded by the German Federal Ministry for Education and Research under grant number 01HQ0522.

The following subsections describe the key design elements of our markets, i.e. the contracts that were traded, the trading mechanisms, the incentive schemes, the group of traders, and the trading software in more detail.

Contracts

In total, we ran 19 markets – 16 markets for the 16 matches in the final rounds starting with the round of sixteen, two markets to predict the tournament's top goal scorer, and the so called championship market where shares of all the 32 national teams taking part in the FIFA World Cup 2006 were traded. These three types of markets are also shown in Table 14 with some more information on the types of contracts available for trade in each of the markets, market start and end time, as well as information on how the contracts were valued at the close of the market (payoff).

Type of market	**Number of contracts**	**Payoff**	**Start time**	**End time**
Championship	1 per country (32)	World champion: 50 Vice-WC: 30 Semi-finals: 20 Quarter-finals: 10 Round of 16: 5 Otherwise: 0	May 15th 2006	July 9th 2006
Match	3 per match: team A wins, team B wins, tie after 2nd half	Event occurred: 10 Otherwise: 0	2 days before the matches	At the end of the matches
Goal scorer	Fluctuating	Top goal scorer: 100 Otherwise: 0	June 6th 2006	July 9th 2006

Table 14: Markets operated during the FIFA World Cup 2006

In case of the first type of markets, namely the championship market, the 32 contracts of the national soccer teams were valued as follows at the close of the market: 50 virtual currency units for the world champion, 30 for the runner-up, 20 for all the teams dropping out in the semifinals, 10 for those dropping out in the quarter finals, and 5 for all those dropping out in the round of 16. All shares of the remaining 16 teams were worthless in the end. The championship market started about three weeks before the first match of the FIFA World Cup 2006 and was closed immediately after the final on July 9th 2006. It was the only market which was online for the complete time period of the world championship.

More than 1,260 traders submitted orders to this market and in total there were more than 80,000 trades. The total number of trades per contract is depicted in Figure 12. Among the most heavily traded contracts are mainly traditional soccer powers such as France, Germany, Brazil, and Argentina. One reason for the relatively high number of trades in the case of "Angola" could be that contracts in the order input mask were sorted alphabetically and the contract of Angola was thus listed first.

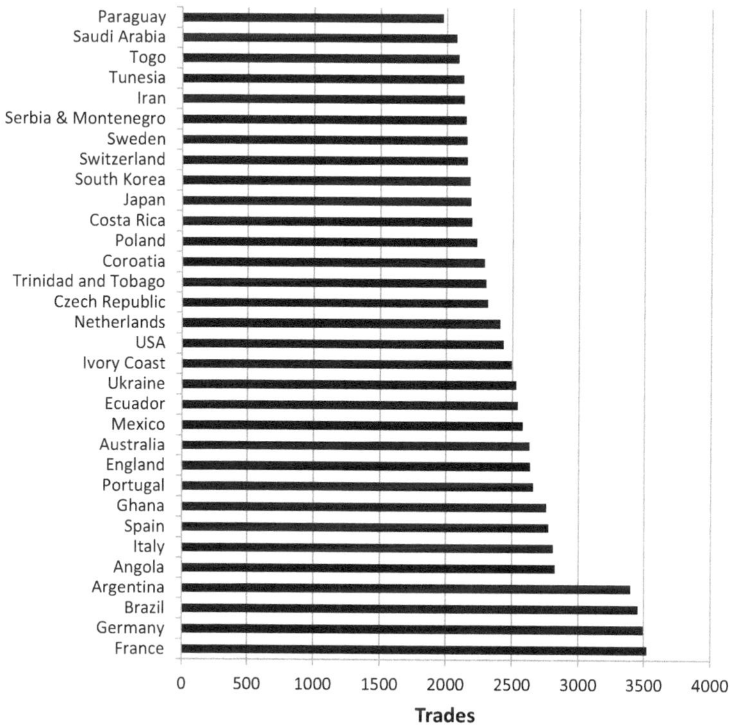

Figure 12: Number of trades in the championship market

The second type of markets, namely the match markets, focused on predicting the outcome of matches in the final rounds. For the 16 matches in the final rounds there were three contracts per match. This is because the following three possible outcomes for every match were defined: Either one of the two national teams won or there was a draw after the second half. The third contract ("draw") was introduced although there were no draws possible in the final rounds of the tournament. The reason for this was that overtimes and penalty shootouts were not considered as their outcomes can be regarded as more or less unpredictable. This is also rather common in case of sports betting with professional bookmakers. Trading started two days before the matches and was stopped immediately after the second half of the matches. The contract corresponding to the event that actually occurred was valued at 10 virtual currency units after the match; the other two contracts were worthless.

Data on the trading activity in the 16 match markets is given in Figure 13 which shows the number of traders as well as the number of trades per match market. On average, there were about 110 traders per market who submitted orders during the two days the markets were open. With 120 trades only "Switzerland-Ukraine" was the match with the smallest number of trades. The most liquid market was the semi-final "Portugal-France" with nearly 900 trades. On average, there were about 450 trades per match market.

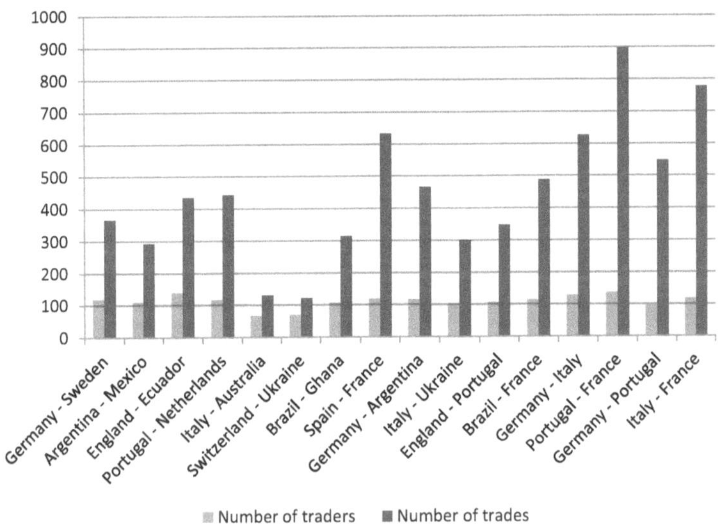

Figure 13: Trading activity in the match markets

The idea behind the third type of markets, namely the two goal scorer markets, was to predict the top goal scorer of the whole tournament. The contract of the top goal scorer was valued at 100 virtual currency units; all other contracts were valued at 0. If there were several top players with the same number of goals, these would have been valued at 100 virtual currency units divided by the number of those players. Initially, the goal scorer market was started with a pre-determined set of players on June 6th 2006. Additionally, there was a contract "other", which was split into two contracts as soon as a player which had so far not been traded in the market scored his third goal. In this case, a contract corresponding to the new player was introduced to the market. If a trader had shares in "other" in his deposit at this point in time, he received an additional contract of the new player automatically.

In order to study the impact of the trading mechanism on the prediction accuracy and the trading behavior there were two goal scorer markets – one market with a continuous double auction and a second market with a call auction. Traders were free to choose any of the two markets for buying and selling their contracts in individual players.

Figure 14 depicts the number of trades over time in both markets.

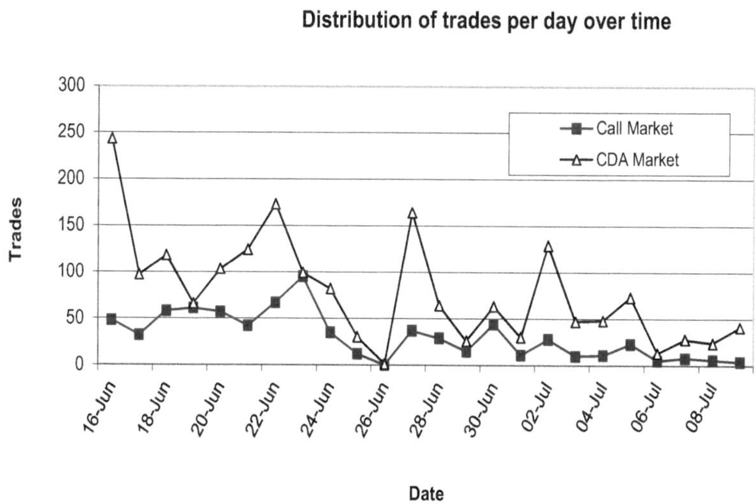

Figure 14: Distribution of trades per day over time

It is obvious that the trading activity measured by the number of trades per day was higher in case of the CDA market than in the call market. On average, there were more than 78 trades per day in the CDA compared to 31 trades per day in the call auction. In total, there were 1886 trades in the CDA market compared to 738 trades in the call market. For some reason (probably immediacy of trading) traders seem to prefer trading in the CDA market. Looking at the number of traders that had at least one trade in the respective market the CDA market with 197 traders also outnumbers the call market with 179 traders.

Trading Mechanisms

Concerning the financial market design, two different trading mechanisms were used in STOCCER – continuous double auctions (CDA) and a call auction. These two trading mechanisms were already roughly explained earlier. The only non-CDA market was one of the two goal scorer markets. Since this market is of no particular importance for answering the research questions addressed in this work it is not described in more detail. All of the other markets, i.e. the championship market, the 16 match markets, as well as the second goal scorer market, employed a CDA in combination with limit orders.

Upon registration each trader was assigned 100 shares of each contract traded in any of the markets as well as a cash account of 100,000 virtual currency units and was thus able to trade instantly. Additional shares were issued by means of so called basic portfolios (Forsythe et al., 1992, Weinhardt et al., 2006b, Weinhardt et al., 2005). A basic portfolio contains one share of every contract which is traded in the respective market. The portfolio price equals the sum of the payoffs for one share of every contract in a market and was e.g. 10 virtual currency units in case of the match markets. It thus corresponded to the payoff for correctly predicting the outcome of a match. Buying and selling portfolios from and to the market operators was therefore risk free for traders and possible at any time while the markets were operating.

Traders submitted offers to buy (bids) or offers to sell (asks). Bids and asks were maintained in queues with a price/time priority, i.e. they were first ordered by price and then by time. Offers remained in the queues until (i) they were withdrawn by the traders, (ii) their lifetime as defined by the trader had expired, or (iii) they were matched with a counter offer. The trades were automatically executed as soon as bid and ask prices in the respective queues were overlapping. When a bid was submitted at a price equal to or exceeding the current minimum price in the ask queue, a trade was executed at the ask price. Analogously, when a sell offer was submitted at a price equal to or less than the current maximum price in the bid queue, a trade was executed at the bid price. In case there were two or more offers at the same price, the earliest offer submitted to the market was executed first. Since the system did not analyze the traders' identities a trader could also trade against himself. Short sales were disallowed by the system. Moreover, submitting offers with insufficient funds in the cash account as well as offers to sell when the trader's portfolio did not contain the corresponding number of shares in a contract were prevented (no short trades).

Incentives

In contrast to traditional betting exchanges for sports events the prediction market STOCCER was operated as a play-money market. Setting up a real-money sports prediction markets is currently not legal in Germany. Instead of investing real money every trader had an initial endowment of 100,000 virtual currency units as well as 100 shares of each contract. The only extrinsic incentives for traders to join the market and reveal their expectations were a ranking of their user names on the STOCCER web page and a lottery of prizes. The overall TOP-100 traders, i.e. the 100 traders with the highest deposit value after the final of the FIFA World Cup on July 9th 2006, took part in a final lottery where the first prizes were shares of the "Garantiefonds UniGarant Deutschland (2012)" investment fund with a value of 3,000, 2,000, and 1,000 Euro. Traders thus had a rather strong incentive to be among the 100 traders with the highest deposit value. In addition, we weekly raffled an iPod among the 20 most active traders of the preceding week.

The most successful trader was able to increase his deposit value by almost 900% between May 15th 2006 and July 9th 2006. At the other extreme, several traders lost almost 100% of their initial deposit value. General terms and conditions were used to prevent traders from creating multiple user accounts and trading against themselves in order to transfer cash from one account to another. Traders were not allowed to register more than once. Furthermore, the use of any kind of software for automated actions was prohibited. Several traders violated these terms and conditions and were disqualified.

Traders

Participation in STOCCER was voluntary. In total, more than 1,700 traders enrolled in the prediction market. During the registration process traders provided information about their gender, age, and country of origin. Traders were predominantly male and quite young compared to the total population of their countries of origin. Almost 89% of the traders were male. Table 15 shows the traders' age distribution. Traders of age 30 and younger account for almost 57% of the total number of traders.

Age	Number of traders	Proportion of traders	Year of birth
<= 20	96	5.26%	>= 1987
20-25	486	26.64%	1982-1986
26-30	454	24.89%	1977-1981
31-35	232	12.72%	1972-1976
36-40	155	8.50%	1967-1971
41-45	137	7.51%	1962-1966
46-50	111	6.09%	1957-1961
51-55	69	3.78%	1952-1956
51-60	38	2.08%	1947-1951
>= 60	46	2.52%	<= 1946

Table 15: Age distribution of traders

Since STOCCER was operated and made known in Germany traders coming from this country also formed the largest group of traders. Overall, traders originated from 72 different countries around the world. As can be seen in Figure 15 about two thirds of the traders were German.

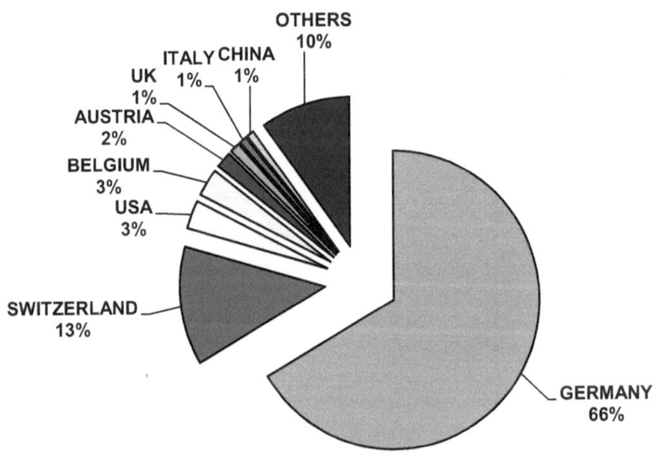

Figure 15: Traders' country of origin

Other countries with a substantial number of traders were Switzerland (235 traders), USA (56 traders), Belgium (55 traders), Austria (33 traders), UK (20 traders), China (15 traders), and Italy (15 traders).

After the FIFA World Cup all of the traders were asked to complete a brief web-based survey to provide descriptive information amongst others about their knowledge and interest in soccer as well as their experience in securities trading. 74 traders completed this survey. Three quarters of these traders saw 16 or more matches during the FIFA World Cup live on TV. 13 out of the 74 traders saw even more than 45 matches on TV during a period of four weeks only. Thus, they seem to be rather enthusiastic about soccer. Several traders also appear to be rather experienced in securities trading. More than 55% of the traders who completed the survey hold a portfolio of securities and about 10% of them trade quite a lot in financial markets, i.e. they conduct more than 20 transactions per year. 27% of the traders completing the survey were even familiar with the concept of prediction markets and had already participated in other prediction markets.

Trading Software

In addition to the key design elements of the STOCCER prediction market described in the previous section one also has to design the web-based trading software as well as the facilities provided for obtaining information about the traders' accounts, the different markets, offers, and trades from a technical point of view. STOCCER had to meet numerous functional and non-functional requirements such as running several prediction markets simultaneously, each of them in multiple languages, or enabling different trading mechanisms for different markets. A fairly flexible platform was needed since it should be easy to reuse in other fields of application such as e.g. market research. Due to the large number of users the software platform also had to be scalable.

In order to fulfill all the requirements the STOCCER trading software was based on two existing trading platforms and thus integrated the functionality of these systems. The two platforms were the political stock market PSM[27], a field-tested platform which was in the past primarily used for predicting the outcomes of political elections (cp. Gandar et al., 1998, Pope and Peel, 1989), and meet2trade[28], a generic electronic trading platform that

[27] http://psm.em.uni-karlsruhe.de
[28] http://www.meet2trade.com

realizes innovative trading features such as bundle trading and enables traders to individually configure their own electronic market (2002). The most liquid market, i.e. the championship market, was operated based on the PSM while all the match markets and the goal scorer markets were run with the meet2trade trading platform. Depending on the market a user wanted to trade in he was forwarded to a trading screen provided by either of the two trading platforms.

The traders of course should not take notice of the fact that STOCCER was built on two existing platforms. Thus, a web interface with exactly the same look and feel for both trading platforms was implemented. An example of the main trading screen is shown in Figure 16.

Market information available to traders included the accumulated bids at the highest three bid prices, the accumulated asks at the lowest three ask prices, the last trading price, and charts showing the price history of all contracts. Moreover, a short description of the market comprising the respective payoff function was shown as part of the trading screen. An alert service informed traders via e-mail in case individual price limits which had been predefined by the respective trader were exceeded. Available account information for individual traders included the number of shares held in each contract, the balance of the cash account, the total value of their deposit, a list of outstanding buy and sell orders, as well as a list of trades.

A ranking of all the traders sorted by their deposit value, i.e. the balance of their cash account plus the value of the contracts they held at the specific point in time, was not part of the trading screen but was separately displayed on the STOCCER web portal www.stoccer.com. This portal also provided more information on the prizes traders could win, the operational principle of the prediction market including a tutorial and frequently asked questions, as well as up-to-date soccer news related to the FIFA World Cup 2006. All the information from the trading screen and the portal was available in four languages, namely German, English, French, and Spanish.

Figure 16: Trading screen of STOCCER

Because the PSM and meet2trade are not based on the same technology, the two trading platforms were integrated on the database level. As can be seen in Figure 17 both systems accessed the same PostgreSQL database. All the required data such as user data was shared by the PSM and meet2trade, so that a trader had to register only once and was then granted access to both of the underlying trading platforms. The dividing rule between the two platforms was the type of contract which was traded. This means that contracts traded in the championship market – which was operated based on the PSM – were not at the same time traded in other markets run by meet2trade and vice versa. Nevertheless, the traders' deposits had to be integrated because both platforms made use of the same cash account. Coordinating the trading activity was consequently required in the sense that e.g. the total volume of a trader's buy orders in both systems was not allowed to exceed the amount of money in his cash account. Both trading platforms also provided market administration tools, e.g. for adding new markets and contracts.

As Figure 17 shows the common PostgreSQL database[29] was operating on one physical machine and was accessed from the two machines which were used to run the two trading platforms PSM and meet2trade (m2t). The STOCCER web portal was built up using the TYPO3 Content Management System[30] and ran on a fourth machine. A separate MySQL database[31] was used to store the content of the portal.

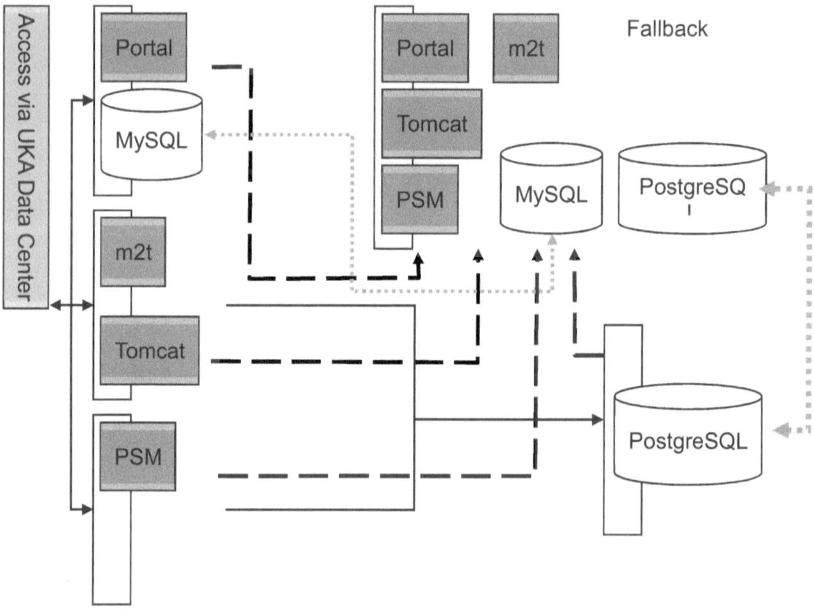

Figure 17: Hardware and software architecture of STOCCER

Running these software systems on four different machines was required to cope with the system load. In order to guarantee the continuous operational availability of the STOCCER trading software a fifth machine was ready to take over the tasks performed by one of the four other machines at any time. For this purpose the data from the two databases had to be replicated on the fifth machine, because the data might otherwise be lost forever or at least be temporarily unavailable.

[29] http://www.postgresql.org/
[30] http://typo3.org/
[31] http://www.mysql.com/

4.2.1.3. Prediction Accuracy

This section provides evidence of our markets' prediction accuracy in the field of sports forecasting. Earlier empirical research substantiates the predictive power of markets relative to traditional forecasting methods such as expert opinions or polls in various fields of application. Data collected from the play-money prediction market STOCCER for the FIFA World Cup 2006 is used to empirically compare the prediction accuracy of sports prediction markets to (i) random predictors, (ii) predictions that are based on historic soccer data about the success of national soccer teams, as well as (iii) betting odds from professional bookmakers.

The idea behind using these three benchmarks is the following: Forecasts of prediction markets are driven by the traders' information and expectations. These forecasts are worthless if they do not result in better predictions than randomly drawing possible outcomes. Thus, random predictors are used as a first benchmark to evaluate the prediction accuracy of the STOCCER markets. Beside historic data, traders also consider current information available to them as well as ongoing developments within the course of the tournament. Using predictions based on the historic success of national soccer teams as a second benchmark allows for examining whether markets are superior to these predictions by incorporating additional information. Within the scope of this research, the FIFA world ranking[32] is used as it is calculated based on pure historic data. Betting odds serve as a third benchmark since they are well-established in sports and known for being very efficient (Schmidt and Werwatz, 2002). Fixed-odds betting differs from prediction markets since the odds are determined by experts, i.e. the bookmakers, and bettors can only decide whether or not to place a bet at the given price. In prediction markets, in contrast, prices reflect the traders' aggregated expectations and can be changed by any trader with deviating expectations.

Description of the Data

The data we are using for our comparison includes the relevant STOCCER championship and match markets as well as betting odds from two major betting companies, the FIFA world ranking, and a random predictor. The two companies providing the betting, namely ODDSET and wetten.de, are used as a benchmark for the STOCCER prediction markets (for a similar approach see (Spann and Skiera, 2009). ODDSET[33] is Germany's largest

[32] http://www.fifa.com/worldfootball/ranking/
[33] www.oddset.de

betting institution and is run by the state-owned lottery. Wetten.de[34] is a popular sports betting provider that is privately held. Both bookmakers offered fixed quotes which bettors could wager against at the time of the FIFA World Cup 2006. A typical betting screen of wetten.de is depicted in Figure 18.

The comparison based on this data differs from the study of Schmidt and Werwatz (2002) in several respects. One of the key features of the soccer prediction markets studied by Schmidt and Werwatz was the real-money investment which was required: every trader had to deposit a certain amount of money (up to 50€) and thus could suffer monetary losses. As such, these markets were similar to the Iowa Electronic Markets, which have proven to be accurate in the past. In the STOCCER play-money markets, however, traders were not required to make any real-money investments. Traders could therefore neither lose nor win any money by revealing their expectations. Another difference is that the STOCCER prediction markets were more liquid than the markets described by Schmidt and Werwatz. Moreover, in addition to comparing the markets' predictions to betting odds and random predictors as done by Schmidt and Werwatz, the following sections also investigate whether the STOCCER prediction markets outperform forecasts that are based on historic soccer data and to what extent predictions based on different types of contracts diverge.

STOCCER Match Markets

There were 16 match markets in STOCCER which focused on predicting the outcome of matches in the final rounds. There were three contracts per match. Either one of the two national teams won or there was a draw after the second half. The contract corresponding to the outcome that actually occurred was valued at 10 virtual currency units while the other two contracts became worthless. The matches, the outcome of the matches, and the trading prices of the three possible outcomes are depicted in Table 16.

The trading prices shown in Table 16 are prices of the last trade before kick-off. According to the efficient market hypothesis, these prices incorporate all relevant information available to the traders at this time. For the comparison of forecasting methods, the predicted outcome of a match in case of the match markets is the one with the highest trading price out of the three possible outcomes. In 9 out of the 16 matches, the contract with the highest trading price corresponded to the actual outcome.

[34] www.wetten.de

Match	Last Trading Price			Result
(Team 1 – Team 2)	Team 1	Draw	Team 2	(Team 1 – Team 2)
Germany – Sweden	9.00	0.30	1.60	2-0
Argentina – Mexico	8.28	2.79	1.91	1-1
England – Ecuador	8.75	3.89	2.00	1-0
Portugal – Netherlands	5.40	1.00	4.40	1-0
Italy – Australia	8.90	0.99	1.99	1-0
Switzerland – Ukraine	7.53	1.50	2.40	0-0
Brazil – Ghana	9.50	0.70	0.70	3-0
Spain – France	3.50	1.30	4.99	1-3
Germany – Argentina	6.00	3.75	3.50	1-1
England – Portugal	3.76	2.70	4.05	0-0
Italy – Ukraine	6.70	2.35	1.04	3-0
Brazil – France	6.16	3.22	3.67	0-1
Germany – Italy	5.10	2.28	3.50	0-0
Portugal – France	2.50	3.49	4.92	0-1
Germany – Portugal	5.90	2.50	2.16	3-1
Italy – France	4.50	3.19	3.91	1-1

Table 16: Last Trading prices of STOCCER match markets

STOCCER Championship Market

Another set of predictions for all the matches can be derived from the contract prices of the competing teams in the STOCCER championship market. Contracts of all 32 national soccer teams were traded in this market. The matches, the outcome of the matches, and the trading prices of the two teams playing the corresponding match are depicted in Table 17. Again, the trading prices shown in Table 17 are prices of the last trade before kick-off. These prices should incorporate all relevant information available to the traders at this time.

Table 17: Last Trading prices of the STOCCER championship market

Match	Last Trading Price		Result
(Team 1 – Team 2)	Team 1	Team 2	(Team 1 – Team 2)
Germany - Costa Rica	19.99	2.17	4-2
Poland - Ecuador	5.47	2.85	0-2
England - Paraguay	13.48	2.93	1-0
Trinidad & Tobago - Sweden	1.15	7.97	0-0
Argentina - Ivory Coast	16.30	4.30	2-1
Serbia & Montenegro - Netherlands	2.61	11.84	0-1
Mexico - Iran	7.15	2.20	3-1
Angola - Portugal	2.10	7.29	0-1

Match	Last Trading Price		Result
(Team 1 – Team 2)	Team 1	Team 2	(Team 1 – Team 2)
Australia - Japan	3.26	4.20	3-1
USA - Czech Republic	3.62	8.05	0-3
Italy - Ghana	13.49	1.99	2-0
South Korea - Togo	3.80	1.64	2-1
France - Switzerland	10.31	6.65	0-0
Brazil - Croatia	31.35	4.88	1-0
Spain - Ukraine	8.00	5.19	4-0
Tunisia - Saudi Arabia	3.10	1.43	2-2
Germany - Poland	19.95	2.22	1-0
Ecuador - Costa Rica	5.35	2.00	3-0
England - Trinidad & Tobago	14.20	1.10	2-0
Sweden - Paraguay	6.61	3.51	1-0
Argentina - Serbia & Montenegro	17.05	1.75	6-0
Netherlands - Ivory Coast	11.20	5.20	2-1
Mexico - Angola	7.45	0.65	0-0
Portugal - Iran	7.62	0.31	2-0
Czech Republic - Ghana	12.10	1.25	0-2
Italy - USA	13.40	0.70	1-1
Japan - Croatia	1.40	5.50	0-0
Brazil - Australia	30.94	4.97	2-0
France - South Korea	10.15	4.85	1-1
Togo - Switzerland	0.85	7.45	0-2
Saudi Arabia - Ukraine	0.96	5.18	0-4
Spain - Tunisia	13.75	0.86	3-1
Ecuador - Germany	6.41	20.99	0-3
Costa Rica - Poland	0.04	1.00	1-2
Sweden - England	6.50	13.50	2-2
Paraguay - Trinidad & Tobago	0.03	2.70	2-0
Portugal - Mexico	8.02	5.00	2-1
Iran - Angola	0.06	1.82	1-1
Netherlands - Argentina	11.25	25.10	0-0
Ivory Coast - Serbia & Montenegro	0.06	100.00	3-2
Czech Republic - Italy	7.70	11.20	0-2
Ghana - USA	3.82	2.00	2-1
Japan - Brazil	0.72	29.35	1-4
Croatia - Australia	5.15	4.94	2-2
Saudi Arabia - Spain	0.05	11.55	0-1
Ukraine - Tunisia	6.00	2.30	1-0
Togo - France	0.80	6.50	0-2
Switzerland - South Korea	7.70	4.29	2-0
Germany – Sweden	23.00	5.34	2-0
Argentina – Mexico	28.40	5.04	1-1
England – Ecuador	14.00	5.63	1-0

Match	Last Trading Price		Result
(Team 1 – Team 2)	Team 1	Team 2	(Team 1 – Team 2)
Portugal – Netherlands	8.37	11.60	1-0
Italy – Australia	18.10	6.20	1-0
Switzerland – Ukraine	13.00	7.18	0-0
Brazil – Ghana	30.20	5.70	3-0
Spain – France	13.95	9.99	1-3
Germany – Argentina	28.45	23.00	1-1
England – Portugal	16.20	16.00	0-0
Italy – Ukraine	19.92	12.85	3-0
Brazil – France	31.01	15.29	0-1
Germany – Italy	41.09	25.65	0-0
Portugal – France	27.00	39.99	0-1
Germany – Portugal	19.79	19.79	3-1
Italy – France	42.00	40.00	1-1

For the following analysis, the predicted winner of a match is the team with the higher trading price before kick-off. A draw is predicted whenever the trading prices of two teams are equal. In 38 out of the 64 matches, the team with the higher trading price was the actual winner of the match.

Betting Odds

In fixed-odds betting, one or several professional experts of a betting company set fixed quotes which are usually not adjusted over time. Bettors then accept or reject those bets at some time before the beginning of the respective event. Essentially, in fixed-odds betting information from potentially knowledgeable bettors is not accounted for when determining the odds. Numerous studies have shown that fixed-odds betting markets are efficient (e.g. Cain et al., 2000, Thaler and Ziemba, 1988). For instance, Pope and Peel (2006) develop a linear probability model which incorporates the probabilities of the actual occurrences of the outcomes and the probabilities implicitly quoted by the odd-setters. They then derive several betting strategies and show that no strategy leads to expected positive returns. Nevertheless, some inefficiencies such as the favorite-longshot bias were detected (Forrest et al., 2005). This means that favorites are undervalued and long shots, i.e. outcomes which are very unlikely, are overvalued. For a recent summary of the history of sports wagering see Vlastakis et al. (2006).

In order to avoid losses, betting companies are required to make accurate predictions (Woodland and Woodland, 1994). With large sums of money at stake, the monetary incentive to predict accurately is pronounced and presumably much stronger than in any prediction market since there is no money at stake in play-money markets and usually little money at stake in real-money markets. Forrest et al. (2005) and Schmidt and Werwatz (2002) emphasize the importance of accurate forecasts for bookmakers in fixed-odds betting markets: "If bets are mispriced, the financial consequences for bookmakers may be serious". Although a commission fee of 15-25% is usually charged (Schmidt and Werwatz, 2002) and can palliate possible losses in the short run, under competition, betting companies setting the quotes have a strong incentive to generate accurate quotes. Moreover, one of the bookmakers' aims is to set the quotes in a way that the bettors' investments distribute evenly on all three outcomes because the bookmakers do then not take any risk (Franke et al., 2006, Franke et al., 2008).

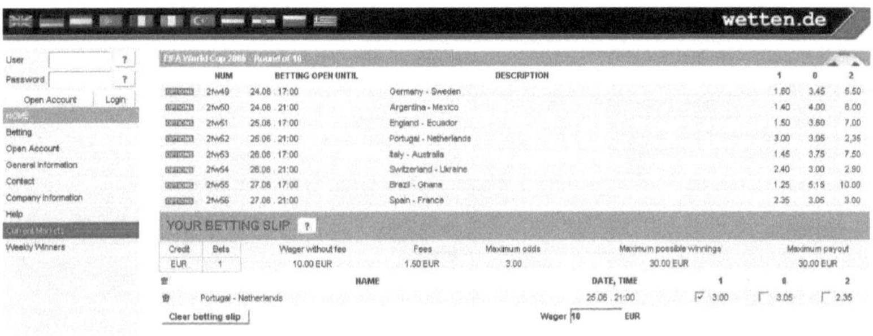

Figure 18: Typical screen of a fixed-odd betting site

For each of the 64 World Cup matches, bets could be placed on a win of the first team (1), a draw (0), and a win of the second team (2). All bets are referring to the score after regular playing time. Extra time and penalty shootouts in the final rounds are not considered. Matches that are not decided within regular time are considered a draw. Betting quotes are stated in decimal odds – a bet quoted with 3.5 pays out 3.5 times the wagering amount in case the corresponding event actually occurs. As bookmakers follow a commercial interest and try their best to avoid short-term losses, the odds include a commission fee. This means that wagering the same amount of money on all three possible outcomes would lead to a 15-25% loss. Since soccer is a popular sport in Germany, one can assume that a considerably large amount of money has been betted on outcomes of matches during the FIFA World Cup 2006.

The matches, the outcomes of the matches, and the quotes from wetten.de are depicted in Table 27 (see Appendix A). Respectively, the data from ODDSET is depicted in Table

28 (see Appendix A). For the following comparison, the predicted outcome of a match is the one with the lowest quote because according to the quotes this is the most likely outcome. For wetten.de, the outcome with the lowest quote corresponded to the actual outcome of the match in 43 out of the 64 matches. For ODDSET, the actual outcome was predicted for 37 out of the 64 matches.

FIFA Ranking

The FIFA world ranking[35] is a ranking system for men's national soccer teams. The teams of the member nations of the FIFA (Fédération Internationale de Football Association) are ranked according to their match results. The most successful team is ranked highest. In the following, the FIFA world ranking is used as another benchmark since it is based on historic data only. Thus, one can investigate whether the STOCCER prediction markets outperform predictions derived from historic data only and hence do not consider up-to-date information about the current status of the national soccer teams such as players dropping out due to medical reasons or due to disqualification.

The FIFA world ranking from May 2006 which is used as a benchmark in the following takes into account the history of the last eight years before May 2006. The ranking is based on the teams' performance, with more recent and more important matches being weighted more heavily in order to reflect the state of the team. It considers the following factors:

- Outcomes of past matches
- Importance of past matches
- Strength of opponents
- Regional strength
- Results in home and away matches
- Number of goals scored

All international "A" matches are relevant for the calculation of the ranking. For each individual factor, points are assigned which are then aggregated to an index value. In

[35] http://www.fifa.com/worldfootball/ranking/

case of most factors complex calculations are used to determine the actual state and strength of the national teams[36].

The matches, the outcomes of the matches, and the ranks of the competing teams in the FIFA world ranking from May 2006 are depicted in Table 29 (see Appendix A). For the following analysis, a win is predicted for the team that has the better position in the ranking. This prediction corresponds to the actual outcome for 30 out of the 64 matches.

Random Draws

Forecasts are worthless if they are not better than randomly drawing one of the possible outcomes. Thus, a random predictor is used as another benchmark to evaluate the prediction accuracy of the STOCCER markets. Since one can observe three possible outcomes per match, an uninformed, random guess would correctly predict 33.33% of the matches. Empirical data supports the hypothesis that the three possible outcomes of a match are equally likely to occur.

Results

In order to compare the prediction accuracy of markets to the other forecasting methods, the hit rate was calculated for each method. The hit rate is the number of correctly predicted matches relative to the total number of predicted matches. How an outcome for a match is predicted in each of the data sets has already been explicated in the last section. Other common evaluation criteria such as the root mean squared error or the mean absolute error for the deviation between the final value of a contract and the last trading price before kick-off cannot be used for comparing the predictions due to the characteristics of the data sets. It is, for instance, impossible to derive probabilities for outcomes of matches from the FIFA world ranking or the trading prices in the championship market. Thus, the hit rate is used as an evaluation criterion which can be employed for all the data sets.

Table 18 compares the hit rate of the different forecasting methods for the whole sample of 64 matches. In case of the STOCCER championship market, a win is predicted for the team with the higher trading price. For the betting odds, the predicted outcome is the one with the lowest quote. The FIFA world ranking predicts a win for the higher-ranked team

[36] The calculation of the ranking is rather complex. Due to its complexity the calculation procedure was changed in the meanwhile. More information on the calculation of the ranking can be found at http://www.fifa.com/mm/document/fifafacts/rawrank/ip-590_10e_wrpointcalculation_8771.pdf.

and in case of the random predictor all three possible outcomes of a match are equally likely to occur.

Method	**No. Obs.**	**Hit rate**	**% improvement**[37]	**p-value**[38]
Championship market	64	59,38%		
Wetten.de odds	64	67,19%	-11,62%	0,203
ODDSET odds	64	57,81%	2,72%	0,799
FIFA world ranking	64	46,88%	26,66%	0,042
Random draw	64	33,33%	78,14%	< 0,001

Table 18: Comparison of prediction accuracy (all matches)

The comparison of the hit rates of the championship market, the betting odds, the FIFA world ranking, and the random predictor for all 64 matches shows that the championship market indeed yields a higher hit rate than the FIFA world ranking and the random draw model. The difference in the hit rate of the prediction market and these two other forecasting methods is significant in both cases (Pearson's chi-square test, p-value < 0.05)[39]. The predictions can thus be improved when using a prediction market instead of these two methods. Table 18 shows the percentage of improvement when one replaces the respective alternative method with a prediction market.

With regard to the hit rate, the betting odds from wetten.de and ODDSET perform similarly well as the predictions derived from trading prices before kick-off in the championship market. Wetten.de slightly outperforms the championship market whereas ODDSET performs almost equally well compared to the market. The difference in the hit rate, however, is not significant in both cases. This can be considered as a success for the prediction market because the prediction accuracy obviously is similarly good as in case of betting odds. This is even more astonishing as the market was a play-money market and was also used to predict the course of the entire tournament instead of focusing on the prediction of the outcome of individual matches.

[37] Percentage of improvement of match market over alternative forecasting method
[38] Chi-square test for difference to hit rate of match market
[39] For more information on Pearson's chi-square test see e.g. Cowan MANN, H. B. & WHITNEY, D. R. 1947. On a test of whether one of two random variables is stochastically larger than the other. *Annals of Mathematical Statistics,* 18, 50-60.

Moreover, the likelihood of draws is systematically underestimated in the championship market. Based on the trading prices in the championship market, a draw would only be predicted if the prices of the competing teams were exactly the same – which is rather unlikely. This also holds for the FIFA world ranking where a draw would only be predicted if two teams were ranked equally.

For this reason, Table 19 compares the prediction accuracy of the various forecasting methods for only those matches out of the total 64 matches which did not end in a draw. In this case, there are only two possible outcomes.

Method	**No. Obs.**	**Hit rate**	**% improvement**[40]	**p-value**[41]
Championship market	47	80,85%		
Wetten.de odds	47	89,36%	-9,52%	0,138
ODDSET odds	47	78,72%	2,71%	0,711
FIFA world ranking	47	63,83%	26,66%	0,003
Random draw	47	50,00%	61,70%	< 0,001

Table 19: Comparison of prediction accuracy (all matches without draws)

The betting odds were adjusted to ignore the probability of a draw by predicting the winner based on which team had the lower odds for it winning the match. However, this does not change the results compared to Table 18. Although again not statistically significant, wetten.de still performs a little better than the championship market while ODDSET is marginally beaten by the market. Also, the championship market still has a much higher hit rate than the FIFA world ranking and the random draw model.

In STOCCER, there were match markets for the 16 matches in the final rounds of the FIFA World Cup 2006. In case of the match markets, the outcome with the highest trading price out of the three possible outcomes is the predicted outcome. Table 20 compares the predictions of these 16 match markets to the predictions of the other forecasting methods.

---

40 Percentage of improvement of championship market over alternative forecasting method

41 Chi-square test for difference to hit rate of championship market

Method	No. Obs.	Hit rate	% improvement[42]	p-value[43]
Match markets	16	56,25%		
Championship market	16	37,50%	50,00%	0,131
Wetten.de odds	16	43,75%	28,57%	0,313
ODDSET odds	16	43,75%	28,57%	0,313
FIFA ranking	16	25,00%	125,00%	0,012
Random draw	16	33,33%	68,77%	0,044

Table 20: Comparison of prediction accuracy (final rounds)

For the last 16 matches of the tournament, the hit rate of the match markets is significantly higher than the hit rate of the FIFA world ranking and of the random draw model. Interestingly, the hit rate is higher in case of the match markets than it is when predicting a win for the team with the higher trading price in the championship market. One reason for this tendency could again be the fact that the likelihood of draws is underestimated in the championship market. Furthermore, traders in match markets can focus on the outcome of one match at a time instead of trying to predict the course of the entire tournament. In the final rounds, the match markets also seem to outperform the betting odds of wetten.de and ODDSET – although the difference is not statistically significant. Moreover, with only one hit fewer, the prediction accuracy of the championship market is again very close to the prediction accuracy of the betting odds.

Altogether, the STOCCER markets are about as accurate as betting odds and more accurate than the FIFA ranking and a random predictor. At first sight, it is somewhat surprising that the hit rate for the championship market, the betting odds, and the FIFA world ranking is on average lower for the last 16 matches than it is when taking into account all 64 matches. However, this is plausible since it should be easier to predict the outcome of matches at the beginning of the tournament than at the end. At the beginning, there are numerous underdogs and clear favorites whereas towards the end of the tournament the performance of teams will not differ that much. Thus, it is presumably much more demanding to predict the outcome of matches taking place in the last rounds compared to earlier matches.

[42] Percentage of improvement of championship market over alternative forecasting method
[43] Chi-square test for difference to hit rate of championship market

4.2.1.4. Arbitrage Opportunities

In the case of STOCCER the markets predicted the outcome of the matches quite accurately. Prediction markets should work well, if they are efficient. In efficient markets, in turn, one does not expect arbitrage opportunities to be persistent. This section, therefore, investigates whether pure arbitrage opportunities existed in one specific market, namely in the STOCCER championship market. This market was chosen for the following analysis, since it was the most liquid market and the only market which was running continuously over a time period of several weeks. Other aspects of market efficiency such as how fast newly arriving information is incorporated into trading prices are not considered here.

In the STOCCER championship market, there are two combinations of trades that can potentially yield arbitrage profits: Firstly, buying all the 32 contracts traded in the market and selling a basic portfolio or, secondly, buying a basic portfolio and selling all the contracts separately in the market. In the first case, one gets paid off on exactly one contract with certainty. If the total of the ask prices on all the contracts of a portfolio is less than the fixed price of the portfolio (200 currency units for STOCCER) at any point in time, an arbitrage opportunity is available by buying n shares of each contract and selling the resulting n portfolios at the fixed price. Instead of selling a basic portfolio a trader can also hold the shares until the end. In the second case, the arbitrage opportunity is present if the sum of all the 32 bid prices is more than 200 currency units.

Figure 19 shows the movement of the sum of bid and ask prices (bid price ≡ offer to buy, ask price ≡ offer to sell) in the STOCCER championship market over time. Most of the time the ask prices sum up to more than 200 currency units. Contrariwise, the sum of the bid prices is in the majority of cases lower than 200 currency units. As was already mentioned above, an arbitrage opportunity exists if the sum of bid prices exceeds or the sum of the ask prices falls below 200 currency units. However, extremely small arbitrage opportunities are presumably not of interest for traders because they do not yield any profit worth mentioning in comparison with the effort which is required to trade a portfolio and 32 contracts.

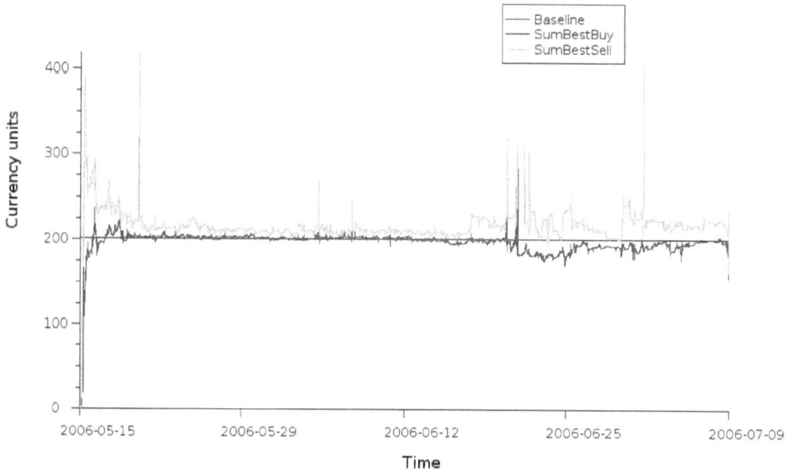

Figure 19: Sum of bid/ask prices in championship market over time

When tolerating arbitrage opportunities of up to one percent of the value of a basic portfolio, i.e. two currency units, there were a total of 229 instances in which an arbitrage opportunity was present between May 15th and July 9th. The arbitrage chances lasted, on average, for about 47 minutes. When tolerating arbitrage opportunities of up to ten percent of the value of a basic portfolio, the number of instances in which an arbitrage opportunity is present declines to seven instances which lasted for 11 minutes on average. Thus, with increasing sums of money at stake the number of arbitrage opportunities declines and substantial arbitrage opportunities are quickly corrected.

Given that trading in this market was relatively thin compared to financial stock markets, it is interesting that the arbitrage opportunities were rather quickly corrected by the traders – provided that a substantial amount of (virtual) money was at stake. All in all, the STOCCER championship market appears to have been efficient in the sense that there were few substantial arbitrage opportunities available by trading basic portfolios or simply holding shares until the outcome was known.

4.2.1.5. Market-Making Traders

Market liquidity can also become a problem in prediction markets since trading is in many cases relatively thin compared to financial stock markets. If markets are rather illiquid, however, new information is not immediately reflected in trading prices and traders might in consequence lose interest in the markets. One observation worthy of note in case of STOCCER is the emergence of market making traders, i.e. traders who provide liquidity by offering to buy and sell a substantial number of shares of a specific contract at the same time. Market makers add to the liquidity and hope to make profit due to the spread between the buying and selling price.

In the following, the threshold for the number of shares which have to be offered on the buy and sell side at the same time in order to qualify as a market-making trader is 50. Furthermore, taking into account whether the corresponding buy and sell orders were submitted within a given time frame can be seen as an additional constraint. Short time frames imply that traders acted as market makers on purpose. To give an example, it is very unlikely that a trader forgot about a sell order or has completely different information when he submits a buy order for the same contract only a little later.

In the STOCCER championship market[44], on average, there are 622 active traders and 72 market-making traders per contract. The number of market makers decreases if corresponding buy and sell orders have to be submitted within a shorter time frame in order to qualify as a market maker. In the following, the time frame is one hour to be considered a market-making trader. In this case, 7.6 per cent of the active traders are regarded as market makers on average across contracts.

In total, there are 289 different market makers. Some traders are acting as market makers for multiple contracts. Six traders, for instance, qualify as market making traders for more than 25 and up to 31 out of the 32 contracts. Table 21 shows the number of traders who are acting as market makers for multiple contracts. All in all, buying and selling the same contract at the same time seems to be a common trading pattern for some of the traders.

#Contracts	**1-5**	**6-10**	**11-15**	**16-20**	**21-25**	**> 25**
#MM (1h)	203	42	20	13	5	6

Table 21: Traders acting as market makers for multiple contracts

[44] This section again relies on data from the championship market since it was the most liquid market and the only market which was running continuously.

Market-making traders are on at least one side of the trade in 81 per cent of the total contracts traded and account for 85 per cent of the trading volume[45]. The number of trades as well as trading volumes per contract increase with the number of traders who qualify as market makers for a specific contract[46]. Figure 20 shows the correlation between the number of market makers and the number of trades. The correlation coefficient of 0.827 indicates a high correlation between those two numbers[47]. With a correlation coefficient of 0.875, the correlation between the number of market-making traders and trading volumes which is depicted in Figure 21 is similarly high[48].

Hence, both correlation coefficients are high and could reflect the fact that additional market-making traders increase liquidity. However, an alternative explanation could be that the factor which generates trading interest also encourages market makers to trade in the corresponding market.

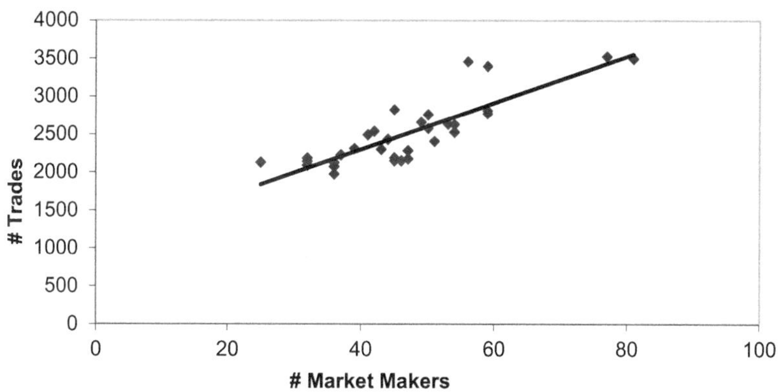

Figure 20: Correlation between number of market makers and number of trades

[45] The market makers' share of trades and trading volume per contract can be found in Table 30 (see Appendix A).
[46] The number of market makers, the number of trades as well as trading volumes per contract can be found in Table 31 (see Appendix A).
[47] Spearman's rank correlation coefficient, p-value < 0.001. For more information on Spearman's rank correlation coefficient see Hotelling and Pabst
[48] Spearman's rank correlation coefficient, p-value < 0.001

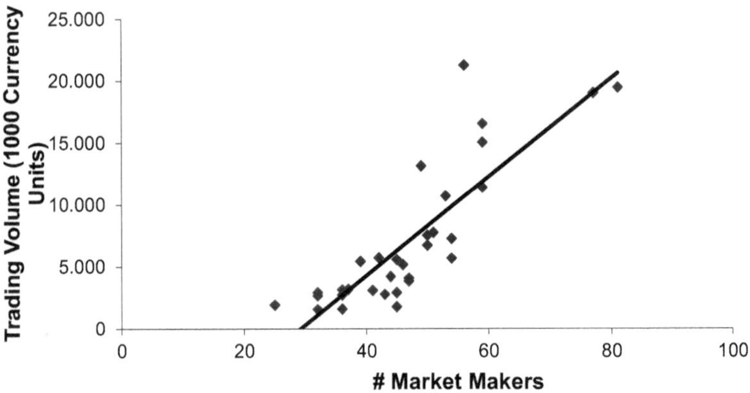

Figure 21: Correlation between number of market makers and trading volume

Without much doubt market makers expect to make profits with their trading strategy of buying and selling specific contracts at the same time. Table 5 shows the market-making as well as the other traders' deposit value, i.e. the sum of the cash and the value of the contracts they hold, at the time when the FIFA World Cup was over and the market had been closed. The average deposit value of market makers is 183,976.52 currency units compared to 135,073.69 currency units for all the remaining traders. The difference between the two groups of traders with regard to the deposit value is significant (Mann-Whitney U test, p-value = 0.003)[49]. Market makers thus are more successful than the remaining traders with respect to their deposit value.

	MM	**Non-MM**	**p-value[50]**
Mean number of trades	413.62	43.21	< 0.001
(Standard deviation)	(719.56)	(61.55)	
Mean deposit value	183,976.52	135,073.69	0.003
(Standard deviation)	(165,738.49)	(62,443.13)	

Table 22: Trading activity and trading success of market makers

[49] For more information on the Mann-Whitney U test see Mann and Whitney
[50] The p-values are obtained from a Mann-Whitney U test.

As shown in Table 22, market-making traders are also trading a lot more than other traders. On average, market makers trade about 414 times whereas other traders only make about 43 trades. Again, the difference in the number of trades is significant. Market makers obviously try to profit from illiquidity. Thus, they play an important role in prediction markets by providing liquidity and consequently allowing for continuous trading.

4.2.2. PSM – The Political Stock Market

This section introduces the Political Stock Market (PSM) platform. After a description of the software itself and its architecture, we present results from three selected markets that allow us to discuss specific aspects of prediction markets, namely fraud, manipulation, and the speed with which markets react to external events relevant to their subject. As we will show using data from the soccer Euro'08 market, prediction markets are able to quickly absorb external events in their prices.

The PSM software has its roots at the Wirtschaftsuniversität in Vienna, where it was developed as a diploma thesis project and first deployed in the 1998 Austrian presidential elections. It has been in use at the Universität Karlsruhe (TH) since 2001, where it was completely rewritten in 2004. The core market component was later used as one of the market engines for the project STOCCER.

4.2.2.1. Software Platform

The original software used a distributed blackboard design with several processes linked via a Linda tuple space (Gelernter et al., 1985). The tuple space allowed each process to write messages (e.g. offers) as tuples to the blackboard and to search for tuples addressed to the process. Each share in the market had its own process managing the order books and trader accounts in this share. In addition, a portfolio process coordinated the primary market. This architecture permits to distribute the different processes over several servers, should the computational load surpass the capacities of a single server.

The backend processes were implemented in C++, the tuple space (Schönfeldinger, 1996) and the web front end in PERL with a CGI interface. While this design allowed a high level of flexibility and distribution, its prototypical implementation had some drawbacks that motivated a complete redesign and reimplementation in 2004. Given the experiences gathered in the operation of the old version, the requirements for the new software included:

- Parallel operation of several markets.
- Customization of the interface for each market or group of markets.
- Easy internationalization.
- Data base backend for consistency through transactional guarantees.
- Implementation of a full accounting system for an easy analysis of the trading data.
- Performance.
- Extensibility for different market mechanisms.

For the data base PostgreSQL was chosen as it offers both transactions and good performance with large data sets. The platform was implemented in PHP because it allows fast development, offers good flexibility, and experienced programmers for this language were available at the time of the reimplementation.

The general architecture follows a MVC pattern. The model is stored in the PostgreSQL data base. The data base contains – in addition to the administrative tables for users, groups, permissions, etc. – a full accounting system that describes the evolution of each trader's accounts. Therefore, the consistency of the system can easily be verified at every point in time, and the state of the market can be reconstructed for each point in time. This allows researchers to analyze the data a posteriori without need for a priori definition of the aspects of the market that should be logged for the analysis.

The view is implemented using the Smarty template engine and PHP. For the interface, the software offers the widgets (order book, trading mask, prices, graphs, etc.) in separate classes such that composition of screens, i.e. web sites, is easy. Furthermore, it is possible to embed single widgets in external web sites via AJAX or IFRAMEs.

The controller is equally implemented in PHP. The market functionality, i.e. mainly matching and execution/accounting is offered by a set of PHP classes that inherit their interface from an "abstract" class `Market`. New market mechanisms are introduced by implementing a descendant class of `Market` and inserting it into the code tree. In addition, the software offers a cron-like functionality for markets that are externally triggered: For instance, clearinghouse markets need such a trigger for the time at which matching is to take place.

Since its reimplementation, the software has served over 150 markets with up to 2000 users per market, and it currently offers 12 different locales.

4.2.2.2. PSM and Irregular Activities

Since the first markets, a special focus in research and operations has been on the subject of fraud and other irregular activities. It became clear early on that this attention is indeed justified. The first market on the original platform was organized for the 1998 presidential elections in Austria, where five candidates (Thomas Klestil, Heide Schmidt, Gertraud Knoll, Richard Lugner, and Karl Walter Nowak) ran for presidency. The market was operated in an academic environment with relatively few users, in contrast to other markets operated by the mass media that drew massive attention from the public. What made this election and the associated markets interesting from the fraud perspective is the candidacy of Richard Lugner who ran as an outsider against Thomas Klestil. While the internal PSM outperformed even the traditional polls with respect to its predictive power, the other, public markets suffered from massive bias in favor of Lugner's share price. With a final price of 9.9 per cent, the share was traded in many markets with for as much as 20 per cent. This surprising prediction resulted in a large number of articles about Lugner as well as many appearances in TV talk shows, resulting in a huge publicity effect. Later, we will discuss this problem class in more detail using data from the 2007 federal Swiss elections.

The second problem predominant in markets where participation is free of charge is fraud: Traders that register several accounts and transfer money between them. This case was clearly observable for instance during the market for the 2004 Ukrainian presidential elections that we will describe in the next section.

4.2.2.3. Fraud: The 2004 Ukrainian Presidential Elections

For the 2004 presidential elections in the Ukraine, a series of markets was operated in cooperation with the Institute for Economic Research, Kiev, and Dolovaya Nedelya, a local newspaper. This series of markets was intended as an experiment on the functioning of prediction markets in emerging democracies, where polls might still be forged and where free news coverage is often hindered. In this setting, the PSM offered an independent channel for the unbiased exchange of opinions. The opening times of the three markets can be found in Table 23.

Round	**Opening**	**Closing**
First round	Sept. 9 2004	Oct. 31 2004
Second round	Sept. 9 2004	Nov. 21 2004
Repetition of the second round	Dec 12 2004	Dec. 26 2004

Table 23: Opening and closing times of markets

The repetition of the second round had become necessary after the opposition accused former president Yanukovich of having forged the official results. Concerning the role of prediction markets in emerging democracies we note that the discrepancy between forecast and official (manipulated) result in the second round was uncommonly high with a RMSE of 5.78. The RMSE in the first round had been 2.30, and 3.69 in the repetition, which is still high.

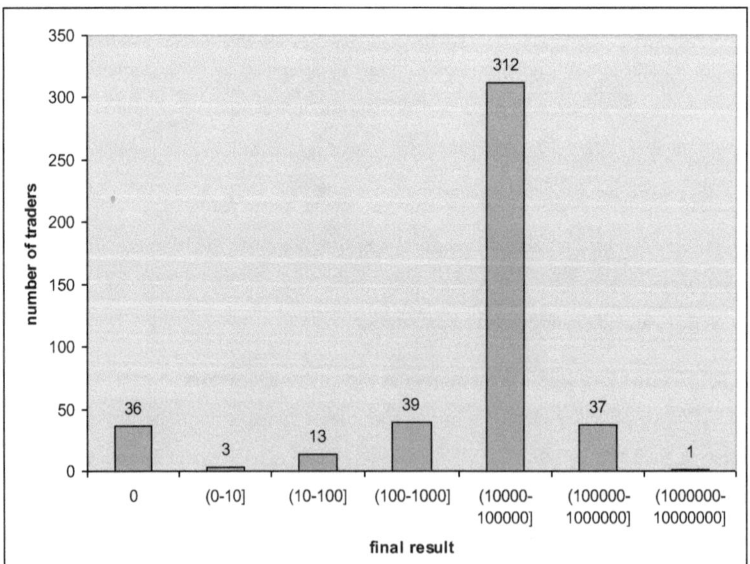

Figure 22: Distribution of final depot values (final result) in the second round

However, the main reason why these markets were included here is the massive amount of fraud that took place in them. Already the first visual impression of the histogram of the ranking (based on the market prices) in Figure 22 gives reason to suspect irregular activities in the market. The original endowment that each trader obtained upon entering the market was 100,000 monetary units, and the winner had accumulated 5.7 million monetary units, in other words, had achieved a performance of 5,700 per cent when the market closed. On the other side of the spectrum, 36 out of 441 traders had lost their entire endowment which is practically impossible in a regular election market.

Another reason for suspicion are the high fluctuations in the share prices as depicted in Figure 23. These two facts point to the presence of fraud in the market. We will see in the following example why this is the case.

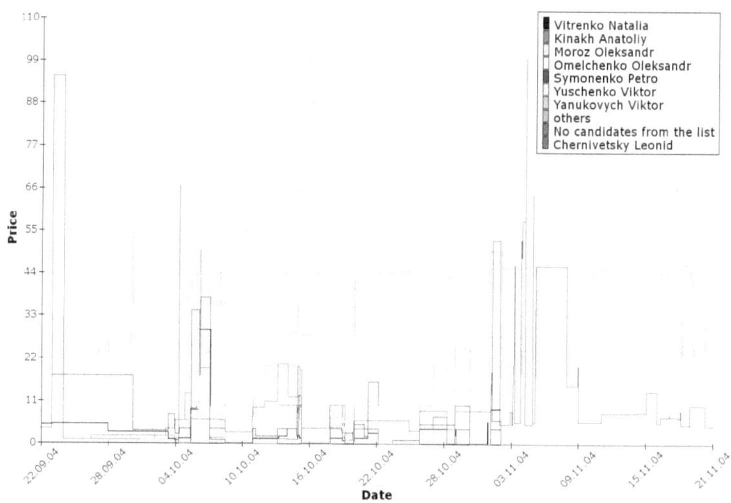

Figure 23: Prices during the second round market

The typical fraud pattern in these markets consists of a trader registering several accounts, a central one and n satellites, each of which receives the full initial endowment of 100,000 monetary units for free. In total, the trader then controls $(n+1)$*100,000 monetary units. In order to transfer the money from each of the satellites to the central account, the central account may start by placing a sell offer infinitesimally below the cheapest sell offer in the order book. This offer is subsequently accepted by the satellite account. The satellite then offers to sell the same shares infinitesimally above the current best buy offer in the order book, and the central account accepts this offer. For an example of this pattern, consider Table 24: The price at the beginning depends on the last trade executed before. After this transaction, a total of 100*(24.99-20.01) = 488 monetary units has been transferred, and the price shows considerable fluctuations.

Optionally, one of the traders can first accept all offers from the order book to widen the spread and thus realize a larger leverage with each of the following transactions.

Action	*Best Buy*	*Cheapest Sell*	*Price*
Start	10 for 20	15 for 25	?
C puts order: Sell 100 shares for 24.99	10 for 20	100 for 24.99	?
S puts order: Buy 100 shares for 24.99	10 for 20	15 for 25	24.99
S puts order: Sell 100 shares for 20.01	100 for 20.01	15 for 25	24.99
C puts order: Buy 100 shares for 20.01	10 for 20	15 for 25	20.01

Table 24: Typical fraud procedure

This behavior is undesirable for two reasons: First, the deliberate dilation of the bid-ask spread and the fluctuations resulting from this form of irregular behavior decrease the stability of the price signals. Other traders therefore perceive more noise, and it becomes more difficult to separate meaningful signals of honest traders from this noise. Second, fraud is indirectly detrimental to the overall quality of the forecast by damaging the incentive system: Often, fraudulent traders occupy the first ranks in the trader ranking with an advance that makes it very hard for traders with regular market activity to catch up. In this case, honest traders may have the impression that they do not have a chance to advance to a winning position in the ranking, and therefore either cease their trading activities or become fraudulent themselves. In both cases, the incentive system has lost its effect, and the information private to these traders is not made public by the market. In total, the performance of the market will suffer.

The Ukrainian markets were the first markets where this problem occurred in this dimension. In the aftermath, organizational measures were taken in order to make this kind of fraud more difficult. In addition to allowing only one account per email address, email verification was introduced, such that with an account registration, the system sends an email with an activation link to the associated email address that contains an activation link. The user must use this link to activate his account and start trading. While not perfect, these measures have reduced the number of fraudulent accounts considerably.

More advanced techniques for the detection have been developed since based on methods from the area of social network analysis (1998). More details on this subject can be found in Schröder (2009).

4.2.2.4. Manipulation: The 2007 Federal Swiss Elections

Another type of irregular behavior – a more critical one – was clearly observable in the 2007 market covering the federal Swiss elections. The market was operated in cooperation with the Swiss newspaper Neue Zürcher Zeitung (NZZ). The shares available for trading are given in Table 25 together with the prices at the closing time of the market, the official results and the prediction errors. The standardized prices are normalized to a sum of 100%.

Share	*Election Result*	*Predicted Result*	*Error*	*Squared Error*	*Price standardized*	*Error (std.)*	*Squared error (std)*
SVP	29.00	25.25	-3.75	14.06	25.32	-3.68	13.54
SP	19.50	20.50	1.00	1.00	20.55	1.05	1.10
FDP	15.60	14.82	-0.78	0.61	14.86	-0.74	0.55
CVP	14.60	14.40	-0.20	0.04	14.44	-0.16	0.03
GP	9.60	10.00	0.40	0.16	10.03	0.43	0.19
GLP	**1.40**	**5.75**	**4.35**	**18.92**	**5.76**	**4.36**	**19.01**
EVP	2.40	2.91	0.51	0.26	2.92	0.52	0.27
Others	7.90	6.11	-1.79	3.20	6.13	-1.77	3.13
Total			12.78	38.25		12.71	37.82
Average			1.60	4.78		1.59	4.73

Table 25: Prices and prediction errors, federal Swiss elections 2007

As can be seen, the market price for the small GLP differs considerably from the election result. This is due to massive manipulation in the market by what we conjecture were supporters of this party.

The basic pattern for price manipulations consists of a fraudulent trader F offering to buy a massive amount of shares for a price that is substantially higher than the common expectation in order establish this price in the market. Alternatively, when the goal is to lower the price of a given share, the trader will offer large numbers of shares for a price lower than the common expectation. The motivation in both cases is to send a signal containing false information to the market, manipulating the opinions of the other traders. In the context of elections, the motivation may be to activate or attract other supporters of the party or to deter supporters of competing parties. Figure 24 shows the relation between buy (cyan, upper curve) and sell (yellow, lower curve) offers for the GLP share over time. As can be seen, there is a massive surplus of buy offers (magenta, middle curve) at nearly all times, and a closer inspection of the data reveals that this surplus was generated by relatively few accounts.

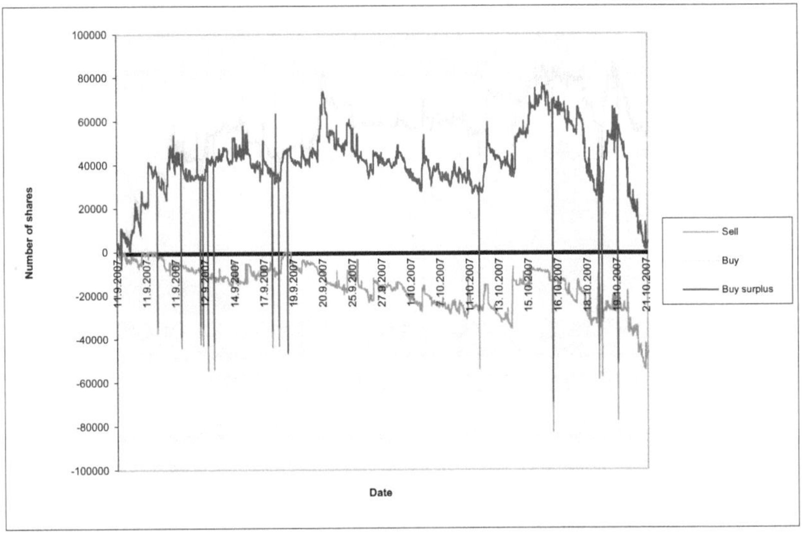

Figure 24: Buy-sell ratio

Seen purely in the context of the incentive system of the market, this behavior is not rational as it induces – possibly massive – losses for the manipulator. Therefore, manipulation must be seen in the context of a supergame. In this supergame, the losses incurred in the market are more than compensated by the gains in other parts of the game, i.e. in real life. In the case of the aforementioned presidential candidate Lugner, the monetary losses in the market induced a publicity value that was a multiple of these losses. In the case of the GLP, there were no monetary losses since the market access was free of charge. The gain here was media attention which might translate to slightly better results in the elections.

A critical aspect of this kind of manipulation is that it not only influences the price of the manipulated share, but also has reverberations on the other shares via the portfolio mechanism and arbitrage traders: Given a market in an equilibrium state, and without arbitrage opportunities (i.e. the sum over all shares of the best buy offers is below 100% and the sum of the cheapest sell offers above 100%), manipulations of this type tend to introduce opportunities for arbitrage trading. In the case of an upward manipulation, the presence of high buy orders will usually raise the sum of the cheapest buy offers over 100%. At this point, arbitrage traders will buy portfolios in the primary market for 100%, and sell the shares contained therein separately, realizing a risk-free profit. This arbitrage trading continues until the sum of the best buy offers is below 100% again. However, since the number of shares asked for by the manipulator is substantial, this implies that the price of at least one other share is lowered due to its best offer being matched completely and removed from the order book. In the case of the Swiss market, this effect mainly concerned the shares of SVP and the share "others", since their buyers did not post buy offers with an accurate price in a sufficient number.

This type of manipulation is especially difficult to compensate by the forces of the market if, as was the case here, the share to be manipulated either has a low price and the price is artificially increased, or has a high price and the price is decreased by manipulation. For an explanation, consider a trader F trying to push the GLP price to 6 who will first accept all sell offers with a price lower or equal to 6. Afterwards, F will place a buy offer for a massive amount of shares. If, in the first phase, he has accepted offers for a total of, say 10,000 monetary units, a total of 90,000 units remains for this purpose, corresponding to a buy offer over 15,000 shares at price 6. Usually, an honest trader H would seize the opportunity and accept as big a part of the buy offer as possible, since he expects the final payoff of the GLP share to be much lower than the price he can realize now on the market. However, in order to sell the shares, H will usually have to buy portfolios first, each costing 100 monetary units. Assuming no other activities on his part, H can therefore acquire a maximum of 1,000 shares of GLP (among with the other shares), that are sold to F, giving H 6,000 monetary units. For these, only 60 portfolios can be bought, and so on. Finally, H ends up having sold 1063 GLP shares, owning as many shares representing the other parties and 60 monetary units. In normal circumstances, H will not be willing to trade the other shares since the sum of their prices is smaller than his expectation for the sum of payoffs, which follows from the expectation for the GLP price and an assumed absence of arbitrage opportunities. As a consequence, H can no longer counteract F's activities, and so it takes a total of about 15 honest traders to neutralize F's manipulations.

What aggravated this situation further was that the GLP only ran in two of the 23 cantons, resulting in many traders not being able to determine a realistic price for the share. This further reduced the market's self-regulating capacities, as even less traders were available to counteract the manipulations based on their own expectations.

This kind of manipulations can also be detected by analyzing the payment flows in the market and applying SNA methods to the data (Schröder, 2009, Franke et al., 2008).

4.2.2.5. Absorption speed of Events: The Euro '08

One aspect that is difficult to measure in the election use case is the speed with which events relevant to the outcome of the election are reflected in the market prices. This is due to the fact that elections take place in a very complex environment where both the relevance of events to the election result and the time lag between a relevant event (for instance a TV debate) and the absorption of this new information in the price are unknown. Furthermore, events like TV debates can have both an instantaneous and a cumulative effect. The revelation of a scandal yet unknown for instance has an instantaneous effect, whereas the cumulative effect comes from viewers aggregating their impressions during the debate and adapting their estimates accordingly.

In other settings, it is much easier to measure the reaction speed since influence factors are less numerous and feedback time is shorter. In 2008, we conducted another soccer-related market once again in cooperation with the NZZ concerning the question who will win the European championship at Euro '08. While the measurement of the absorption speed of news initially was not in the research focus, it became quickly clear that up to several hundred participants trading during the games provided immediate feedback and absorption of the games' development to the prices in the market. However, the evaluation of reaction speeds in the following will be limited to a minute-based analysis since participants watched the matches using different technologies with considerably different delays between events (goals) and their perception by the user. For instance, viewers receiving an analog terrestric signal learned of goals about 20 seconds earlier than those receiving digital signals. Therefore, using a resolution smaller than a minute for the analysis does not appear to be sensible.

For an example of the absorption speed of the market, consider the graph in **Fehler! Ungültiger Eigenverweis auf Textmarke.** showing the prices during the match Germany-Portugal. Kick-off was at 20:45 MEST. Germany scored first at 21:07, closely followed by a second goal at 21:11. The corresponding prices are given in **Fehler! Ungültiger Eigenverweis auf Textmarke.**. As can be seen, the prices for both teams reacted quite immediately, Germany gaining 7.8 basis points, Portugal losing approximately 12.7 points.

Time	**Price Germany**	**Price Portugal**	**Event**
21:06	11.20	13.68	
21:07	12.67	12.17	1:0
21:08	13.98	10.00	
21:09	14.00	8.00	
21:10	14.95	7.01	
21:11	14.99	8.00	2:0
21:12	15.00	6.10	
21:13	17.40	2.69	
21:14	18.25	2.69	
21:15	18.35	2.00	
21:16	19.00	1.00	

Table 26: Prices during the first two German goals

When Gomes scored at 21:25, prices reacted accordingly, Portugal regaining about three quarters of its losses before returning to the former state at 22:03 when Ballack increased the German score to three goals. The final goal by Postiga at 22:29 is still noticeable in the prices rising from 0.21 to 0.99 for a short period of time; however traders did at this time not have a sufficient confidence in Portugal's ability to change the outcome of the match. As a consequence, prices for Portugal dropped quite quickly until the match ended at 22:36.

This example shows that prediction markets not only have advantages over traditional forms of forecasting in terms of quality, but that they also deliver very current forecasts where polls for instance only take samples in regular intervals. Therefore, prediction markets can detect and show microtrends as well as the reverberations of single events – be it a goal in a soccer match or the announcement of a scandal in political forecasting with unmatched speed.

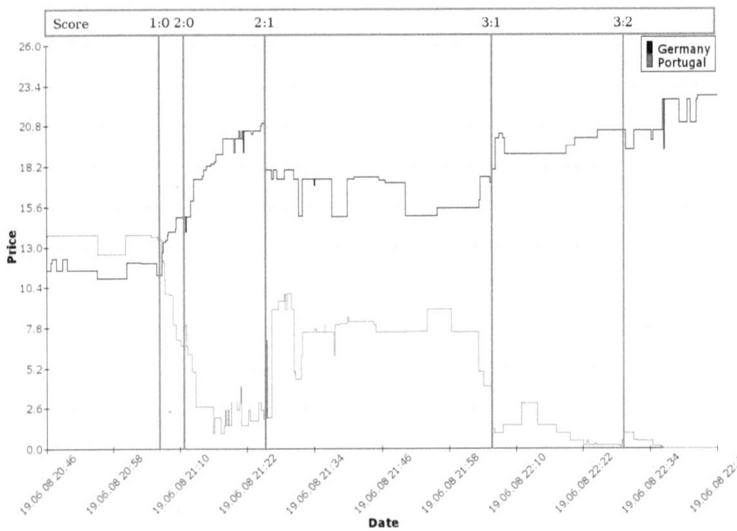

Figure 25: Prices during the match Germany-Portugal

4.2.3. AKX – The Australian Knowledge eXchange

Water availability is a key limiting factor for agriculture across much of Australia. Historically, rainfall is highly variable, and with climate change it is likely to become even more so. As well as impacting agriculture, lack of water harms the environment, reducing the health of streams and rivers, reducing recreational opportunities and values. Water is also a significant issue for urban populations – residents of most towns and cities now routinely face restrictions on water use, for example limiting the watering of gardens, car washing, etc.

Managing water resources is therefore a critical environmental, social and economic issue. Water is stored in dams, and released according to availability and need. Accurate forecasts are a key aspect of water management. Water managers can actively adjust allocations for agriculture, release water for environmental flows or adjust restrictions on urban users. These decisions are guided in part by water use forecasts. Based on work by Stathel et al. (2009) we propose using prediction markets to manage information about water levels in dams.

4.2.3.1. Water Availability in Australia

Good forecasts are also critical to many water users. For example, many farmers in the Murray-Darling basin in south-eastern Australia own the rights to use water for irrigation. The amount of water they actually receive in any given year is calculated based on the amount of water available in dams and other storages. In practice the amount of water they are eligible to access for use will change as climatic and other events impact on the inflows to dams. The actual amount of water they will be eligible to receive will generally remain uncertain at the time they plant their crops, so there is a large element of risk in planting decisions.

A broad range of factors impact dam levels. Rainfall intensity and location, as well as the capacity of soils to intercept and store water (itself a function of evaporation and transpiration) are clearly crucial, along with land-use in the catchments surrounding dams. Demand for water by downstream users and decisions by water managers are also important.

Considerable research is focused on forecasting water availability in Australia including a major effort by CSIRO to develop an integrated Water Resources Observation Network (WRON). A range of hydrological models have been developed which provide scientific guidance for management decisions. However, as dams are impacted by so many actors, from urban households turning on taps to farmers adjusting their land use, no model can ever be fully comprehensive. The general dam level changes following a seasonal periodic pattern. We thus propose the usage of such markets to manage information about water levels in dams. Prediction markets have the potential to integrate the outputs of hydrological models with local knowledge and private information held by water users. Even if they can make even a small contribution to improve water forecasts they can have a large impact. To manage the supply Australia has the highest water storage capacity per capita in the world. Furthermore, due to the utmost importance of water supplies, the Australian government established the National Water Foundation to tackle the severe drought. The Australian states plan to spend 18 billion A$ over the next few years on water infrastructure such as the grid system, dams, desalination and recycling.

Our market covers five well-known dams within the Murray-Darling Basin and can be visited at http://akx.csiro.au. We aggregate information carried by humans directly affected by water availability in south east Australia. The idea behind is that not only experts like meteorologists have relevant information. We therefore involve people who are directly affected and have information about how the weather situation or water demand will change within a short period of time.

Our main research goal is to investigate whether prediction markets are applicable for predicting dam levels. In order to measure "who" holds valuable information we run a public and a specialist market. By setting up two identical markets, we compare the forecast ability of experts and novices. Finally, we compare the predictions which are derived from trading prices with the actual water levels as well as a historic model in order to determine the prediction accuracy of the markets. Subsequently, the design parameters and the functioning of the markets are introduced. Furthermore, we discuss the trading activity and prediction accuracy.

4.2.3.2. Trading Platform

Traders are buying and selling contracts depending on their own estimation of how full or empty the corresponding dams will be at specific points in time. The AKX markets are limited to eight dams in south east Australia. Because the three dams – Bendora, Corin, and Googong – are located in the same region close to the Australian Capital Territory, they are bundled and traded as one stock (ACT). The other four dams are far apart from each other and are thus independent. As a result, the markets offer five contracts to be traded.

The AKX markets were launched in mid-November 2008 and will be operated at least until the end of February 2009 in order to predict dam levels. In total, 98 traders registered with the play-money prediction market. There are payouts at three points in time - 18th December 2008, 22nd January 2009, and 26th February 2009.

Traders were paid out according to the cash and share holdings in their accounts. The trading platform was open to the public 24 hours a day, 7 days a week. The stated goal for each trader thus was to increase her overall holdings by buying contracts when they were undervalued and selling them when they were overvalued – like in financial stock markets. As traders aren't expected to have any prior trading experience, the user interface was created to support their first steps. Aside from the detailed help page a trading wizard was available. The wizard assists traders to convert their expectations of dam levels to prices and quantities at which they may wish to trade. It converts their estimate of the level of a particular dam into a price for that contract. It also asks the level of confidence they have in their estimate, which it uses to suggest a quantity of contracts to trade (The more confidence they have in their estimate, the greater the quantity suggested). It suggests both bids and asks, offering a choice of buy and sell orders.

The more common way to submit orders is the trading screen. As depicted in Figure 26 it features the last transaction, bid and ask prices as well as a trader's own holdings in each stock and available money. When a certain stock is selected, the order book opens. Due to display reasons it is limited to list a maximum of five entries. The system is implemented as a real time trading system, which means that prices and orders are updated automatically without the user reloading the page. In order to provide some historic trading information, charts with price developments of all stocks are available. Additionally current dam levels are displayed next to the current market forecast on the start page and the trade wizard.

Contracts

As described above, 5 contracts were traded in the AKX. On each of three payout dates, all contracts were paid out according to the actual dam levels. So if a dam level was 60% in the end, the pay off for the corresponding contracts was AKX$ 60. If a trader thinks that the dam will be 70% full at the end of the month, for example, she will buy contracts up to a price of 70 AKX$. In total, 38 traders submitted 870 orders to this market which resulted in more than 340 transactions.

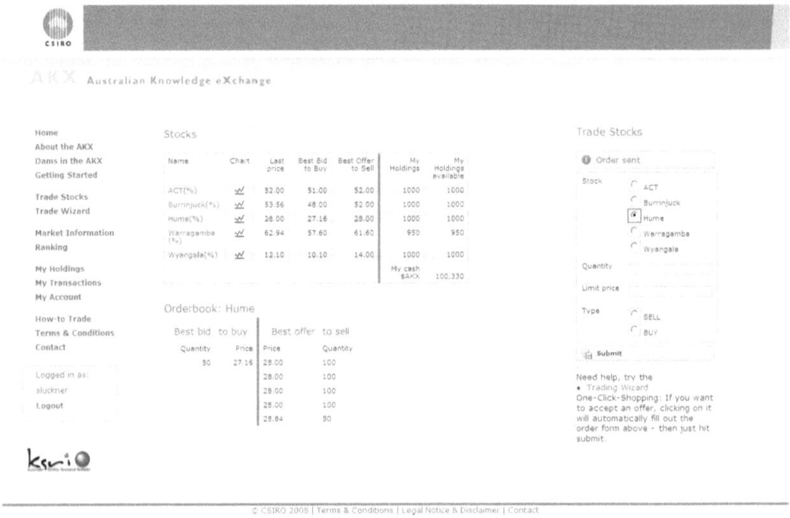

Figure 26: Trading screen of the AKX market

Trading mechanism

The AKX market employed a CDA in combination with an automated market maker. Upon registration each trader was provided with 1,000 shares of each contract and a cash account of 100,000 AKX$ and was thus able to trade instantly. Traders submitted limit offers to buy (bids) or limit offers to sell (asks). Bids and asks were maintained in queues with a price/time priority, i.e. they were first ordered by price and then by time. Offers remained in the queues until (i) they were withdrawn by the trader, or (ii) they were matched with a counter offer. Trades were automatically executed as soon as bid and ask prices in the respective queues were overlapping. When a bid was submitted at a price equal to or exceeding the current minimum price in the ask queue, a trade was executed at the ask price. Analogously, when a sell offer was submitted at a price equal to or less than the current maximum price in the bid queue, a trade was executed at the bid price. In case there were two or more offers at the same price, the earliest offer submitted to the market was executed first.

As we expected a relatively thin market, a market maker mechanism was installed. It was designed to place buy and sell orders above and below the last transaction price to always ensure trading possibilities. In general the last two transaction prices are taken and depending on their difference the next orders' price will be increased/reduced by certain percentages, for example by 20% if the difference is higher than 5 AKX$. More precisely, the market maker mechanism offered buy as well as sell orders at every time. The order volume was 50 shares fixed and the prices were linked up with the last transaction price. Buy/sell orders were offered with a spread of +/- 3% based on the last transaction price. If two consecutive transaction prices differed more than 5 currency units, a jump in the fundamental value is very liable and therefore the market maker cancels old orders and sets new ones with a spread of +/- 20% based on the last transaction price. If the following transaction price is smaller than 5 currency units away from the last price, the spread decreases to +/- 10% and +/- 3% respectively in the next step. If an order from the market maker was only partly executed, the remaining order was deleted and a new one was put based on the new transaction price.

Short sales were disallowed by the system. This implies that submitting offers with insufficient funds in the cash account as well as offers to sell when the trader's portfolio did not contain the corresponding number of shares in a contract were prevented.

Incentives

The AKX market was operated as a play-money market. The only extrinsic incentives for traders to join the market and reveal their expectations were

1) A ranking of their user names on the AKX web page where they could follow their performance compared to all other traders.
2) A list of the five most active and best performing users was shown on the start page
3) A lottery of prizes was given to traders.

The best trader at the payout date won a 50 AUS$ gift voucher. Additionally, two more 50 AUS$ voucher were shuffled between active traders. The probabilities of winning these vouchers depended on the trader's portfolio value. Hence, if a trader has a 10 percent higher portfolio value compared to another trader, his probability of winning a voucher is also 10 percent higher. General terms and conditions were used to prevent traders from creating multiple user accounts and trading against themselves in order to transfer cash from one account to another. Traders were not allowed to register more than once. Furthermore, the use of any kind of software for automated actions was prohibited.

Traders

Participation in the AKX was voluntary. Keeping the registration process simple besides their chosen username, password and real email address, it only requires the users' postal code. It is stated before the registration that generated data will be kept anonymously and other participants can only see the freely chosen user name. The market was advertised in local newspapers and radio stations. Additionally, we sent out private invitations to catchment authorities, meteorologists and farmer organizations. Since the AKX was operated and publicized in Australia the majority of traders were Australian.

Every action of traders was recorded in the AKX market. Full information about the trading activity, i.e. orders and trades, and traders' shareholdings is available or can be calculated for any point in time.

4.2.3.3. Trading Activity and Prediction Accuracy

In this section, we present the results of the market period (2008/11/17 - 2009/02/26). Originally, we planned comparing two identical markets; one with water experts and one open to the public. The expert's response was surprisingly negative, especially hydrologists replied with a number of furious emails. The tenor was that existing models are accurate enough and a 'game' would not be suitable for increasing forecast performance. As a result only three experts registered in the market. Hence, one of our research questions became obsolete and in the following section we compare the public market results with a historic benchmark model.

Altogether, 89 users registered with the public AKX market and 46 of them submitted at least 1 order. The number of traders per contract was nearly equal. Users submitted 415 sell and 419 buy orders and the market maker contributed another 701 orders. These orders resulted in 543 transactions which are also evenly distributed over the five contracts in the AKX.

As depicted in Figure 27 the number of transactions and the resulting trading volume was very mercurial on each trading day. At minimum, we observed 0 trades per day and at maximum we had a trading volume of almost 60.000 AKX$ per day. That peak occurred on the 13th of December. A reminder e-mail was sent out to all participants on the 12th of

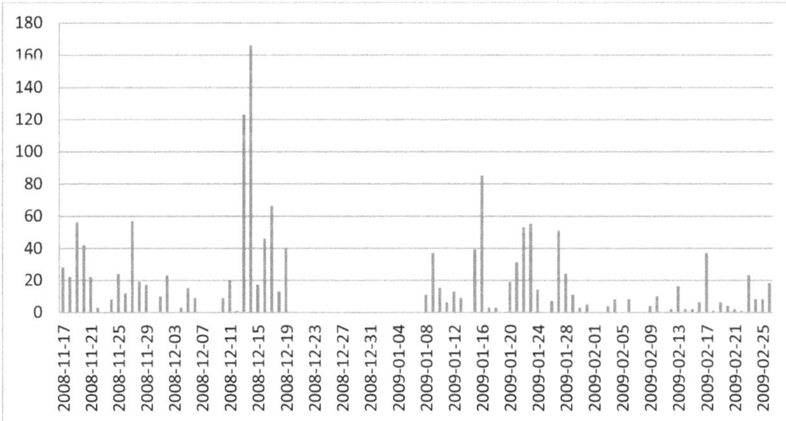

Figure 27: Number of transactions per day

December. As a consequence, the trading activity was 6-7 times higher on the following day than on average. Another two remainder emails were sent out on the 15th of January and on the 23rd of February resulting in slightly higher trading activity on the following days. The traditional Australian summer holidays, Christmas and New Year's Eve led to the 'no-trade' period.

Altogether, the trading activity was quite low. As shown in Figure 27 the number of submitted order continuously decreased over the three periods. In this experiment, prediction markets were used to predict water dam levels. In the first trading period many mistakes happened. For example, one trader mixed up values in the trading screen and this resulted in a short term distortion of market prices. Nevertheless, traders were able map their private information to adjust prices and to predict dam levels in the following trading periods. Figure 28 lists the forecast results compared to the actual dam levels. The solid line represents the perfect forecast. The closer the dots are to that line, the better was the prediction. That type of visualization is called "Calibration" and is commonly used to show the accuracy of markets compared to the actual outcome. The three trading periods are represented with three different symbols. It is easy to see that the second period was the most accurate one followed by the third and the first period.

From each dam, except of the ACT, publicly available historic records are available. Thus, we analyzed these records and developed a "historic" benchmark model based on the average water dam level changes from several years in the past. The results were adapted to the market periods which are represented as crosses in Figure 28 as an additional, independent forecast (H-Model). An interesting result is that traders in the market overestimated low water dam levels. In Figure 28 one can see that between 0 and 30 every market result was overestimated, in contrast in this in interval the historic model was extremely accurate. On the other hand, in water dam levels of 50 and above the market was in sum more precise than the historic model; the cumulated error was lower for the market forecast.

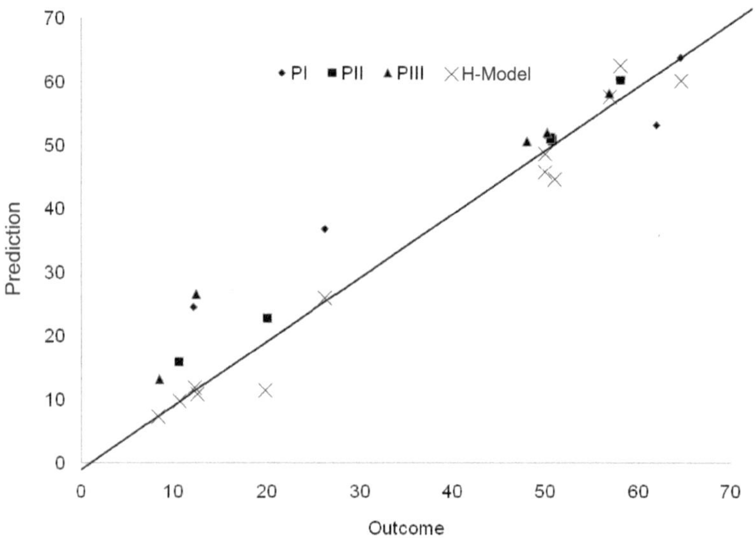

Figure 28: Market prices (i.e. prediction) and final dam levels (i.e. outcome)

The results of the market as well as the historic model can be benchmarked against the outcome. Figure 29 depicts the mean average error of both methods summing up the errors of each period per dam. As already mentioned, there is no historic data for the 'ACT' dams. In Figure 29, the error of the three periods is accumulated for each dam. The market was more accurate than the historic model in two cases (Burrinjuck and Warragamba dams).

In contrast, the historic model beats the market in the Wyangala and Hume dam contracts. We monitored the location of each trader during the registration process and interestingly no active traders actually live close to the Wyangala dam, which showed an error rate of above 20.

We observed that in sum the accuracy of the second market period was with an absolute error of 10.9 more accurate than the historic model with 16.9. Altogether, only the second trading period was more accurate than the historic model. Although we measured the highest trading activity in the first market period, the results of that period were the most inaccurate ones with an error of 25.1 compared to the historic model with 7.7.

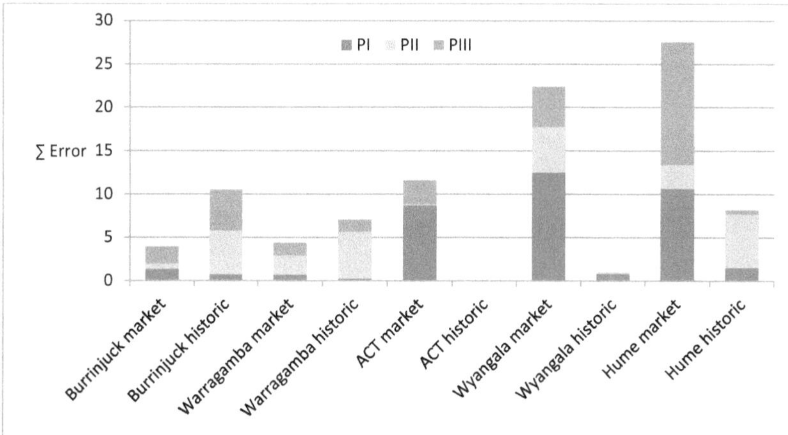

Figure 29: Accumulated Error – Market vs. Historic Model

Typically, information markets in other domains like politics or sports usually show error rates of only a few percent. Often, errors less than one percent in high liquid markets like the US presidential election market are reported. Therefore, the overall performance of the market is poor compared to the previously run markets.

4.2.3.4. Conclusion

Despite the rather poor performance in our market with a small number of observations, prediction markets are a promising method to collect information from a variety of people and can lead to appropriate results in predicting water dam levels. The open issues for further research are to investigate if there were systematic problems in the market design which caused the prediction errors in the AKX. Another question is to test if the incentive scheme for traders was appropriate in order to motivate traders to disclose their private information. Additionally, it would be interesting to see if traders living close to the dams hold superior information compared to other participants living far away from dams. Yet, it remains an open question how the expert's provisos can be addressed. These questions may be special to the application of information markets in the context of natural resource management. A first result of our field experiment is, that information markets can be – with further research and development in the mentioned questions – applicable for environmental predictions.

4.3. Creating Value with Prediction Markets in Service Industries

4.3.1. Service Innovation with Idea Markets

Service innovation is strategically important for service companies (Smith et al., 2007). Due to the increasing importance of the service sector and servitization of products (Rada and Vandermerwe, 1988, Needly, 2007), more attention has been drawn to the innovation process of services that is comparatively little studied (Dolfsma, 2004). According to a Business Week article, service innovation is the "next big thing" (Jana, 2007).

Some services' nature is that of deliverable goods with an intangible aspect of being co-created by the service provider and the customer (Dolfsma, 2004). Service innovation is the process of developing new services for the customer or improving existing services as described by Dolfsma (2004) and Smith et al. (2007). As stated and very similar to product innovation, service innovation can be "complex, time consuming, costly and often unsuccessful". According to Cooper (2001), service innovation starts with the identification of new service ideas and ends with launching them to the market. However, researchers question the notion of a strictly linear process. They describe it as "ad hoc" (Dolfsma, 2004) or "messy" (Smith et al., 2007), for instance.

There is a fundamental tension in service innovation. Innovative services are critical for the survival and growth of service companies, but at the same time the management of new service development is challenging, as 42% of all new services fail in the market place as they do not meet the customers' needs (Griffin, 1997). These failures have a strongly negative financial impact on the service company and can lead to long-term negative consequences (Goldenberg et al., 2001).

The fundamental notion is that the quality of the initial ideas already determines the future market success. Thus, the first tasks in the innovation process are focused; that is idea generation and screening (Smith et al., 2007, Cooper, 2001). Both suffer from a high uncertainty and require long-range forecasting abilities on the future market success as Soukhoroukova et al. (2009) have pointed out for new product ideas, and the same holds true for service innovation. For managing these crucial tasks more successfully, methods are needed to reduce uncertainty and complexity.

Thus, in the context of prediction markets, idea markets as augmented prediction markets with the possibility for participants to propose new ideas are a new promising method for service innovation generation and screening, building up on the ideas of new product development by Soukhoroukova et al. (2009), which we detail further below. This approach is promising as it identifies uncertainty to be a main problem and, at the same time, addresses it. Thus, the idea market concept can be applied for the generation and screening of new services in a similar way as in new product development, because the innovation process does not differ significantly in these tasks. Both, the development of new products and new services starts with the creation of good initial ideas (Dolfsma, 2004, Cooper, 2001), which need to be evaluated, before a decision is made which ideas to pursue (Soukhoroukova et al., 2009).

Idea generation and screening are "crucial initial tasks" (Soukhoroukova et al., 2009) at the fuzzy front-end of the new product and service development process. It is quite comprehensible that the market success of the new services relies on the quality of the initial ideas. Rochford (1991) argues that it is less costly compared to the following stages. She is in line with Goldenberg et al. (2001) who consider idea generation and screening to have the highest point of leverage in the whole innovation process. The earlier poor ideas are screened out, the lower the costs. Thus, idea generation and screening are a very critical step and should be emphasized.

4.3.1.1. Idea Market Concept

An idea market basically builds upon the prediction market concept. Hence an idea market can be understood as an augmentation of a prediction market. According to Soukhoroukova et al. (2009), there are two major distinctions between idea markets and prediction markets: First, the set of contracts in an idea market is variable and dynamic as it consists of the suggestions from the participants. Therefore, the prediction market is augmented with a floatation mechanism. Thus, the participants are no longer presented alternative contracts from a fixed set, but are given the opportunity to create own ideas described as contracts. Then these so called idea contracts are proposed to the market by the participants themselves and can be traded in the market, if the initial investment barrier is overcome. Second, the final contract value has to be determined as it cannot be determined by the outcome of the contract's underlying event, which might never occur (see Section 4.1.2 for a discussion and evaluation of different possibilities to determine the contracts' final values).

Soukhoroukova et al. (2009) propose idea markets as a tool for managing idea generation and screening in order to take advantage from the predictive power of prediction markets. The following considerations show how the idea market concept can be applied for generating and screening of new service ideas.

The Internet-based idea market is able to bring employees from diverse departments with relevant ideas and knowledge together and an extranet might even make the integration of external participants e.g. customers possible. The idea generation is conducted via the floatation mechanism that allows the participants to propose new idea contracts to the market. The basic idea is that each of these contracts describes a new service idea and its price represents its future market success, e.g. the revenues yielded in a prospective year by this particular service or the market share. The scalability of the Internet ensures that a broad search process for new service ideas can easily be conducted as it provides a scalable platform to manage a high number of participants and idea contracts.

The idea market supports the screening of ideas as well as it reduces the ideas subsequently in a multi-step process. After an idea has been proposed, it can be initially screened by a floatation mechanism, in which a lower bound of investments by the remaining participants has to be reached. If the new idea contract reaches the lower investment bound, it is evaluated by the market in a second step. Anticipating the market success of a new service, the participants with diverse expertise then provide their individual assessments through trading decisions. The idea market aggregates all available information and thus provides a prediction through the price. This price can then serve as a basis for decision making which ideas to pursue. Then the decision maker can either adopt the idea market's evaluation or take it into account when he conducts a definite screening.

To conclude, the idea market copes with the complexity of cross-departmental collaboration. It enables the participants to propose their own ideas and evaluate those of others using the market mechanism. That way, the idea market gives structure to the "iterative and 'fuzzy'" (Smith et al., 2007) process of service innovation. Ideas can be proposed when they occur over the whole duration of the market. If once an idea has been proposed it cannot be removed, but improved ideas can be proposed. Thus, service ideas can be evaluated iteratively and continuously be improved. Moreover, as the idea market does not require personal attendance, it is feasible for remote collaboration of large groups, diverse departments, other companies and even international participation at low cost.

4.3.2. Market and Opinion Research

To-date, surprisingly few applications of prediction markets exist for market and opinion research (for a review see (Soukhoroukova et al., 2010)). This is despite the fact that those applications which have been conducted have shown very good forecasting results, along with more advantages. We outline these advantages compared to other market and opinion research methods, such as polls, questioning of experts or conjoint analyses, below, and give examples for further possible applications of prediction markets.

First of all, one significant advantage of prediction markets compared to the other approaches is that they do not require a representative sample of participants to work accurately (e.g., Berg et al., 2001), as participants are asked for everyone's beliefs rather than her or his own believe. Moreover, if not having to rely on a representative sample, much effort can be avoided in choosing the representative sample. Additionally, Christiansen (2007) and Soukhoroukova and Spann (2005) show that reliable forecasts can already be determined with as few as ten or a dozen participants.

Second, because by using a market mechanism for rewarding participants, participants are incentivized to reveal their truthful predictions. In contrast, they are not incentivized to reveal their truthful information in case of e.g. polls, or even when they are experts questioned on a specific topic.

Third, even supposed enough data points from questioning of participants are available, the question of how to aggregate the opinions still remains of how to arrive at one single prediction for a specific event. Simple averaging might in some cases be sufficient, but for instance in case of the underlying data is heavily skewed, averaging might not lead to reliable results. Prediction markets, on the other hand, provide an aggregation mechanism by the use of a market mechanism.

Fourth, the use of prediction markets generally results in lower costs than an alternative market or opinion research method (e.g., Dahan et al., 2009). One important reason is that, as mentioned in the first point, a representative and therewith large sample of participants is not needed, eliminating the need for screening and disbursing a high number of participants.

Fifth, prediction markets scale very with respect to the number of participants or the number of questions asked in the markets (e.g., Dahan et al., 2009). While other methods such as conjoint analysis only work up to an upper bound of questions, prediction markets can be designed in a way that the scalability is virtually infinite.

While these five major advantages show that in contrast to other market and opinion research methods, prediction markets have distinct advantages, we can identify three areas in which services based on prediction markets have future potential besides service innovation (see 4.3.1).

1. *Evaluation of market opportunities*: Prediction markets can be used for the assessment of market opportunities of services in distinct regions of the world or for the forecasting of impacts of the enhancement of existing services. Especially because prediction market participants are not physically tied to a certain world location, but are able to participate online over the Internet, these questions can relatively cheaply be answered for single market segments in any world region. On the other hand, for international services for instance, the scalability of the prediction markets makes a complete international assessment of markets possible.

2. *Forecasting of economic data*: Prediction markets can be used to forecast, for instance, the GDP or economic growth. Based on this information, decisions can be made regarding the market entry in certain regions and countries. This information would be especially crucial if making significant investments in promising markets.

3. *Revelation of regions with market opportunities*: Due to the scalability of prediction markets, the identification of single regions or countries out of a large pool of possible regions or countries, respectively, is possible. This application would be highly beneficial as the assessment and identification of every single possible region or country would be highly costly and therefore often, unfeasible. If the number of

regions or countries, respectively, is very high, an idea market might even be feasible to identify those regions/countries, which presumably have the highest potential.

5. Conclusion

Prediction markets have continuously gained importance in academia and industry over the last couple of years. Nevertheless, it is a rather new field of research and numerous open questions still need to be tackled. There were two main objectives for this work. First, we wanted to discuss the key design elements of prediction markets which are crucial for their successful implementation. Results from several empirical studies reported in this work demonstrate the importance of designing such markets properly in order to derive valuable predictions. Second, we aimed at showing that prediction markets have immense predictive power and that they are useful in a broad field of applications. We thus discussed previous applications of such market in some detail

We believe that prediction markets also have huge potential in other fields of application. Moreover, we do not aim at replacing traditional forecasting methods with prediction markets. We rather believe that markets are a useful tool which should be combined with well-established forecasting methods. Thus, future research should not only try to extend applications of prediction markets in innovative fields but also aim at serving as a useful supplement to existing forecasting methods.

Fields of application

The work at hand provided evidence of markets' prediction accuracy in the field of sports forecasting. So far, most of the research comparing the accuracy of prediction markets to other forecasting methods focused on fields of application where information is dispersed among a large group of traders. Thus, it is interesting to extend this stream of research to other fields of application where relevant information is only available to a limited number of experts and to study how well prediction markets work under such circumstances. This would also allow for examining whether adding uninformed traders to a market with few well-informed experts distorts trading prices and thus harms prediction accuracy.

Combining prediction markets with established forecasting methods

The track record of prediction markets suggests that markets may help to better foresee future developments and trends. Yet, other forecasting methods should not always be replaced by prediction markets. Markets can rather be thought of as a supplement to existing forecasting methods since they can be seen as a tool for continuous monitoring of developments. Moreover, prediction markets are useful to motivate creative thinking and idea generation as well as to identify knowledgeable traders which can afterwards be recruited as experts for alternative forecasting methods such as the Delphi technique.

Prediction markets can also be combined with voting mechanisms or crowd-based innovations. Open Innovation processes, for example, may make use of the *wisdom of crowds* to facilitate crowd sourcing, crowd ranking, and crowd analysis of innovations. The idea is to brainstorm as a community, vote on the ideas to rank them, and then forecast key metrics using a prediction market. Such combinations of several forecasting methods should be considered when aiming at improving a company's foresight capabilities.

Information about the authors

Stefan Luckner has worked on prediction markets as a PhD student and post-doctoral researcher at Universität Karlsruhe (TH), Germany. His research interests were incentives and traders' behavior in prediction markets. Stefan is now working as an IT strategy consultant for a leading management consulting company.

Jan Schröder's research background is formal social network analysis and incentive systems. His main interest laid in manipulative tendencies and actions within networks like prediction markets which he received his PhD for at Universität Karlsruhe (TH). Jan is co-founder of KENFORX, a company providing methods for collective intelligence like prediction markets.

Christian Slamka has mainly worked on prediction market designs, especially trading mechanisms, for his Ph.D. at Goethe University Frankfurt. He is now working as a consultant in strategic IT management projects in the telecom industry.

Markus Franke started working in the field of prediction markets in 2001 at Universität Karlsruhe (TH), where he also received his PhD. His research focused on data analysis and clustering. Markus founded, together with Jan, KENFORX, a company providing methods for collective intelligence like prediction markets.

Andreas Geyer-Schulz worked as a professor for economics in Augsburg and Vienna and is currently a full professor at the Institute for Information Systems and Management at the Karlsruhe Institute of Technology (KIT), heading the group "Information Services and Electronic Markets" (EM). His research interests lie in the formal discussion and math based specification of economic issues. His main working areas are business dynamics, information systems and prediction markets.

Bernd Skiera is a Professor of Electronic Commerce at the University of Frankfurt, Germany, and a member of the board of the E-Finance Lab. His research focuses on prediction market, electronic commerce, online marketing, pricing and customer management. His work has been published in, among others, Management Science, Marketing Science, Journal of Marketing Research, Journal of Marketing, Journal of Management Information Systems, Journal of Product Innovation Management, and European Journal of Operational Research.

Martin Spann is a professor of Electronic Commerce at the Ludwig-Maximilians-University (LMU Munich). He obtained his PhD on prediction markets at the University of Frankfurt in 2002. His research interests are prediction markets, pricing & auctions, online marketing, social network analysis and new product & innovation management.

Christof Weinhardt is professor for Information Management and Systems at the Karlsruhe Institute of Technology (KIT), heading the group "Information and Market Engineering" (IM). His research focus is on interdisciplinary topics related to Market Engineering with applications in IT services, energy, financial, and telecommunications markets. Since 2010 he is expert advisor on the Committee of Enquiry "Internet and the Digital Society" of the Federal Parliament of Germany.

Appendix A

Match (Team 1 – Team 2)	Odds 1	Odds 0	Odds 2	Result (Team 1 – Team 2)
Germany - Costa Rica	1.26	5.45	13.00	4-2
Poland - Ecuador	1.90	3.35	4.40	0-2
England - Paraguay	1.62	3.55	6.45	1-0
Trinidad & Tobago - Sweden	14.00	5.45	1.25	0-0
Argentina - Ivory Coast	1.55	3.75	7.05	2-1
Serbia & Montenegro - Netherlands	4.45	3.30	1.90	0-1
Mexico - Iran	1.55	3.80	6.85	3-1
Angola - Portugal	10.00	4.70	1.35	0-1
Australia - Japan	2.60	3.20	2.80	3-1
USA - Czech Republic	4.45	3.30	1.90	0-3
Italy - Ghana	1.58	3.50	7.35	2-0
South Korea - Togo	2.00	3.25	4.05	2-1
France - Switzerland	1.70	3.35	6.00	0-0
Brazil - Croatia	1.40	4.50	8.50	1-0
Spain - Ukraine	1.85	3.30	4.75	4-0
Tunisia - Saudi Arabia	1.83	3.35	4.80	2-2
Germany - Poland	1.55	3.85	6.70	1-0
Ecuador - Costa Rica	1.82	3.55	4.50	3-0
England - Trinidad & Tobago	1.20	6.50	15.00	2-0
Sweden - Paraguay	1.85	3.40	4.55	1-0
Argentina - Serbia & Montenegro	1.55	3.50	6.50	6-0
Netherlands - Ivory Coast	1.80	3.50	4.70	2-1
Mexico - Angola	1.45	4.35	7.45	0-0
Portugal - Iran	1.35	4.50	8.50	2-0
Czech Republic - Ghana	1.60	3.65	5.75	0-2
Italy - USA	1.45	3.80	7.80	1-1
Japan - Croatia	5.60	3.60	1.60	0-0
Brazil - Australia	1.25	5.20	11.00	2-0
France - South Korea	1.40	4.10	8.00	1-1
Togo - Switzerland	8.75	4.00	1.30	0-2
Saudi Arabia - Ukraine	8.75	4.35	1.35	0-4
Spain - Tunisia	1.30	4.50	10.00	3-1
Ecuador - Germany	7.50	4.25	1.40	0-3
Costa Rica - Poland	4.00	3.30	1.75	1-2
Sweden - England	3.65	2.30	2.55	2-2
Paraguay - Trinidad & Tobago	1.90	3.55	3.30	2-0
Portugal - Mexico	2.40	2.50	3.50	2-1
Iran - Angola	2.55	3.30	2.45	1-1
Netherlands - Argentina	3.40	3.10	2.05	0-0
Ivory Coast - Serbia & Montenegro	1.95	3.40	3.40	3-2

Match (Team 1 – Team 2)	Odds 1	0	2	Result (Team 1 – Team 2)
Czech Republic - Italy	3.55	2.80	2.15	0-2
Ghana - USA	2.20	3.30	2.90	2-1
Japan - Brazil	11.25	5.50	1.20	1-4
Croatia - Australia	2.10	3.30	3.10	2-2
Saudi Arabia - Spain	12.00	5.50	1.18	0-1
Ukraine - Tunisia	1.60	3.60	5.00	1-0
Togo - France	11.00	5.00	1.20	0-2
Switzerland - South Korea	1.90	2.95	3.85	2-0
Germany – Sweden	1.60	3.45	5.50	2-0
Argentina – Mexico	1.40	4.00	8.00	1-1
England – Ecuador	1.50	3.60	7.00	1-0
Portugal – Netherlands	3.00	3.05	2.35	1-0
Italy – Australia	1.45	3.75	7.50	1-0
Switzerland – Ukraine	2.40	3.00	2.90	0-0
Brazil – Ghana	1.25	5.15	10.00	3-0
Spain – France	2.35	3.05	3.00	1-3
Germany – Argentina	2.60	3.10	2.60	1-1
England – Portugal	2.15	3.10	3.35	0-0
Italy – Ukraine	1.55	3.45	6.35	3-0
Brazil – France	1.75	3.20	4.75	0-1
Germany – Italy	2.20	3.00	3.30	0-0
Portugal – France	3.65	3.05	2.05	0-1
Germany – Portugal	1.75	3.40	4.40	3-1
Italy – France	2.50	2.80	3.00	1-1

Table 27: Betting odds from wetten.de

Match (Team 1 – Team 2)	Odds 1	0	2	Result (Team 1 – Team 2)
Germany - Costa Rica	1.20	4.00	9.00	4-2
Poland - Ecuador	1.75	2.85	3.40	0-2
England - Paraguay	1.45	2.90	5.45	1-0
Trinidad & Tobago - Sweden	9.00	4.00	1.20	0-0
Argentina - Ivory Coast	1.50	2.85	5.00	2-1
Serbia & Montenegro - Netherlands	3.60	2.85	1.70	0-1
Mexico - Iran	1.40	3.20	5.20	3-1
Angola - Portugal	7.50	3.50	1.25	0-1
Australia - Japan	1.80	2.90	3.15	3-1
USA - Czech Republic	3.45	2.80	1.75	0-3
Italy - Ghana	2.25	2.75	2.45	2-0
South Korea - Togo	1.30	3.40	6.50	2-1
France - Switzerland	1.55	2.85	4.50	0-0
Brazil - Croatia	1.40	3.10	5.50	1-0
Spain - Ukraine	1.75	2.80	3.50	4-0
Tunisia - Saudi Arabia	1.75	2.80	3.50	2-2
Germany - Poland	1.40	3.10	5.50	1-0
Ecuador - Costa Rica	1.80	2.80	3.30	3-0
England - Trinidad & Tobago	1.15	5.00	10.00	2-0
Sweden - Paraguay	1.75	2.85	3.40	1-0
Argentina - Serbia & Montenegro	1.50	3.00	4.60	6-0
Netherlands - Ivory Coast	1.65	2.80	4.00	2-1
Mexico - Angola	1.30	3.55	6.00	0-0
Portugal - Iran	1.30	3.55	6.00	2-0
Czech Republic - Ghana	1.35	3.25	6.00	0-2
Italy - USA	1.50	3.00	4.60	1-1
Japan - Croatia	1.20	4.00	8.25	0-0
Brazil - Australia	3.60	2.85	1.70	2-0
France - South Korea	1.35	3.25	6.00	1-1
Togo - Switzerland	5.00	3.30	1.40	0-2
Saudi Arabia - Ukraine	1.25	3.50	7.50	0-4
Spain - Tunisia	6.00	3.55	1.30	3-1
Ecuador - Germany	6.00	3.55	1.30	0-3
Costa Rica - Poland	4.00	3.10	1.55	1-2
Sweden - England	3.00	2.35	2.20	2-2
Paraguay - Trinidad & Tobago	1.70	3.25	3.10	2-0
Portugal - Mexico	3.00	2.85	1.90	2-1
Iran - Angola	1.85	2.90	3.00	1-1
Netherlands - Argentina	2.10	2.40	3.10	0-0
Ivory Coast - Serbia & Montenegro	2.40	2.90	2.20	3-2
Czech Republic - Italy	3.25	2.60	1.90	0-2
Ghana - USA	2.00	2.80	2.80	2-1
Japan - Brazil	7.50	4.20	1.20	1-4

Match (Team 1 – Team 2)	Odds 1	Odds 0	Odds 2	Result (Team 1 – Team 2)
Croatia - Australia	2.00	2.75	2.85	2-2
Saudi Arabia - Spain	10.00	4.25	1.15	0-1
Ukraine - Tunisia	1.90	2.60	3.25	1-0
Togo - France	10.00	4.25	1.15	0-2
Switzerland - South Korea	1.50	3.00	4.60	2-0
Germany – Sweden	1.60	3.00	4.00	2-0
Argentina – Mexico	1.35	3.25	6.00	1-1
England – Ecuador	1.35	3.25	6.00	1-0
Portugal – Netherlands	2.70	2.80	2.05	1-0
Italy – Australia	1.40	3.00	6.00	1-0
Switzerland – Ukraine	2.20	2.80	2.50	0-0
Brazil – Ghana	1.20	4.00	8.25	3-0
Spain – France	2.15	2.75	2.60	1-3
Germany – Argentina	2.35	2.75	2.35	1-1
England – Portugal	1.95	2.75	3.00	0-0
Italy – Ukraine	1.45	3.00	5.10	3-0
Brazil – France	1.60	2.85	4.15	0-1
Germany – Italy	1.95	2.75	3.00	0-0
Portugal – France	3.15	2.70	1.90	0-1
Germany – Portugal	1.65	2.90	3.75	3-1
Italy – France	2.30	2.60	2.60	1-1

Table 28: Betting odds from ODDSET

Match (Team 1 – Team 2)	Rank Team 1	Rank Team 2	Result (Team 1 – Team 2)
Germany - Costa Rica	19	26	4-2
Poland - Ecuador	29	39	0-2
England - Paraguay	10	33	1-0
Trinidad & Tobago - Sweden	47	16	0-0
Argentina - Ivory Coast	9	32	2-1
Serbia & Montenegro - Netherlands	47	3	0-1
Mexico - Iran	4	23	3-1
Angola - Portugal	57	7	0-1
Australia - Japan	42	18	3-1
USA - Czech Republic	5	2	0-3
Italy - Ghana	13	48	2-0
South Korea - Togo	29	61	2-1
France - Switzerland	8	35	0-0
Brazil - Croatia	1	23	1-0
Spain - Ukraine	5	45	4-0
Tunisia - Saudi Arabia	21	34	2-2
Germany - Poland	19	29	1-0
Ecuador - Costa Rica	39	26	3-0
England - Trinidad & Tobago	10	47	2-0
Sweden - Paraguay	16	33	1-0
Argentina - Serbia & Montenegro	9	47	6-0
Netherlands - Ivory Coast	3	32	2-1
Mexico - Angola	4	57	0-0
Portugal - Iran	7	23	2-0
Czech Republic - Ghana	2	48	0-2
Italy - USA	13	5	1-1
Japan - Croatia	18	23	0-0
Brazil - Australia	1	42	2-0
France - South Korea	8	29	1-1
Togo - Switzerland	61	35	0-2
Saudi Arabia - Ukraine	34	45	0-4
Spain - Tunisia	5	21	3-1
Ecuador - Germany	39	19	0-3
Costa Rica - Poland	26	29	1-2
Sweden - England	16	10	2-2
Paraguay - Trinidad & Tobago	33	47	2-0
Portugal - Mexico	7	4	2-1
Iran - Angola	23	57	1-1
Netherlands - Argentina	3	9	0-0
Ivory Coast - Serbia & Montenegro	32	47	3-2
Czech Republic - Italy	2	13	0-2
Ghana - USA	48	5	2-1
Japan - Brazil	18	1	1-4

Match	Rank		Result
(Team 1 – Team 2)	Team 1	Team 2	(Team 1 – Team 2)
Croatia - Australia	23	42	2-2
Saudi Arabia - Spain	34	5	0-1
Ukraine - Tunisia	45	21	1-0
Togo - France	61	8	0-2
Switzerland - South Korea	35	29	2-0
Germany – Sweden	19	16	2-0
Argentina – Mexico	9	4	1-1
England – Ecuador	10	39	1-0
Portugal – Netherlands	7	3	1-0
Italy – Australia	13	42	1-0
Switzerland – Ukraine	35	45	0-0
Brazil – Ghana	1	48	3-0
Spain – France	5	8	1-3
Germany – Argentina	19	9	1-1
England – Portugal	10	7	0-0
Italy – Ukraine	13	45	3-0
Brazil – France	1	8	0-1
Germany – Italy	19	13	0-0
Portugal – France	7	8	0-1
Germany – Portugal	19	7	3-1
Italy – France	13	8	1-1

Table 29: Positions of competing teams in the FIFA ranking (May 2006)

Contract	#MM	#MM-TX / #TX (%)	MM-TradVol / TradVol (%)
Angola	45	76.19%	89.51%
Argentina	59	83.34%	82.42%
Australia	54	77.70%	77.33%
Brazil	56	84.26%	87.41%
Costa Rica	45	76.28%	91.46%
Cote d'Ivoire	41	79.21%	87.57%
Croatia	47	83.54%	89.96%
Czech Republic	39	82.04%	86.63%
Ecuador	42	82.66%	87.61%
England	53	85.83%	85.77%
France	77	83.74%	81.98%
Germany	81	81.74%	80.43%
Ghana	50	80.01%	78.31%
Iran	25	76.61%	83.00%
Italy	59	84.62%	83.38%
Japan	32	78.92%	81.28%
Korea Republic	47	81.59%	87.14%
Saudi Arabia	36	79.48%	86.24%
Mexico	50	82.88%	82.12%
Netherlands	51	86.73%	89.22%
Paraguay	36	80.21%	90.10%
Poland	37	79.68%	88.66%
Portugal	49	85.25%	81.73%
Serbia & Montenegro	32	80.16%	90.84%
Spain	59	84.20%	82.56%
Sweden	45	84.98%	87.79%
Switzerland	46	83.03%	85.54%
Togo	32	78.87%	88.60%
Trinidad & Tobago	43	77.54%	81.92%
Tunisia	36	82.02%	94.56%
Ukraine	54	82.24%	82.12%
USA	44	80.55%	82.04%

Table 30: Trading activity of market makers relative to all traders

#MM: Number of market makers

#TX: Number of trades

TradVol: Trading volume

#MM-TX: Number of trades by market makers

MM-TradVol: Trading volume of market makers

Contract	# MM	# TX	Trading Volume
Angola	45	2822	2906207.80
Argentina	59	3397	16518302.03
Australia	54	2628	5669446.43
Brazil	56	3456	21245499.70
Costa Rica	45	2188	1768325.72
Cote d'Ivoire	41	2491	3101242.95
Croatia	47	2284	4051174.70
Czech Republic	39	2311	5415731.57
Ecuador	42	2538	5698810.33
England	53	2633	10684352.88
France	77	3524	19028177.09
Germany	81	3494	19461286.03
Ghana	50	2756	6698774.88
Iran	25	2129	1911784.25
Italy	59	2809	15022296.44
Japan	32	2182	2658963.66
Korea Republic	47	2173	3822122.80
Saudi Arabia	36	2071	1588805.83
Mexico	50	2576	7509094.91
Netherlands	51	2404	7744212.78
Paraguay	36	1971	2717072.52
Poland	37	2224	3173347.09
Portugal	49	2658	13111409.97
Serbia & Montenegro	32	2142	2919919.26
Spain	59	2772	11381556.92
Sweden	45	2150	5552289.44
Switzerland	46	2151	5149225.96
Togo	32	2087	1550324.84
Trinidad & Tobago	43	2297	2770702.86
Tunisia	36	2124	3124018.13
Ukraine	54	2528	7253846.15
USA	44	2432	4209720.01

Table 31: Number of market makers and trading activity per contract

#MM: Number of market makers

#TX: Number of trades

Bibliography

ANTWEILER, W. & ROSS, T. 1998. The 1997 UBC Election Stock Market. *Canadian Business Economics,* 6, 15-22.

BECKMANN, K. & WERDING, M. 1996. "Passauer Wahlbörse": Information Processing in a Political Market Experiment. *Kyklos,* 49, 171-204.

BERG, J. E., FORSYTHE, R., NELSON, F. & RIETZ, T. A. 2001. Results from a Dozen Years of Election Futures Markets Research. *In:* PLOTT, C. & SMITH, V. L. (eds.) *Handbook of Experimental Economic Results.* Amsterdam: Elservier Science.

BERG, J. E., FORSYTHE, R. & RIETZ, T. A. 1996. What Makes Markets Predict Well? Evidence from the Iowa Electronic Markets. *In:* ALBERS, W., GÜTH, W., HAMMERSTEIN, P., MOLDOVANU, B. & VAN DAMME, E. (eds.) *Understanding Strategic Interaction: Essays in Honor of Reinhard Selten.* New York: Springer.

BERG, J. E., FORSYTHE, R. & RIETZ, T. A. 1997. The Iowa Electronic Market. *In:* PAXSON, D. & WOOD, D. (eds.) *Blackwell Encyclopedic Dictionary of Finance.* Oxford, UK: Blackwell.

BERG, J. E., NELSON, F. & RIETZ, T. A. 2003. Accuracy and Forecast Standard Error of Prediction Markets. Working Paper, College of Business Administration, University of Iowa.

BERG, J. E. & RIETZ, T. A. 2003. Prediction Markets as Decision Support Systems. *Information Systems Frontiers,* 5, 79-93.

BERG, J. E. & RIETZ, T. A. 2006. The Iowa Electronic Markets: Stylized Facts and Open Issues *In:* HAHN, R. & TETLOCK, P. C. (eds.) *Information Markets: A New Way of Making Decisions in the Public and Private Sectors.* Washington D.C.: AEI Press.

BOHM, P. & SONNEGARD, J. 1999. Political Stock Markets and Unreliable Polls *The Scandinavian Journal of Economics,* 101, 205-222.

BONDARENKO, O. & BOSSAERTS, P. 2000. Expectations and learning in Iowa. *Journal of Banking and Finance,* 24, 1535-1555.

BRÜGGELAMBERT, G. 2004. Information and efficiency in political stock markets: using computerized markets to predict election results. *Applied Economics,* 36, 753-768.

CAIN, M., LAW, D. & PEEL, D. 2000. The Favourite-Longshot Bias and Market Efficiency in UK Football Betting. *Scottish Journal of Political Economy,* 47, 25-36.

CHAN, N., DAHAN, E., KIM, A., LO, A. & POGGIO, T. 2002. Securities Trading of Concepts (STOC). Working Paper, Massachusetts Institute of Technology.

CHEN, K.-Y. & PLOTT, C. R. 2002. Information Aggregation Mechanisms: Concept, Design and Implementation for a Sales Forecasting Problem. *Social Science Working Paper No.1131.* Pasadena: California Institute of Technology.

CHEN, Y., CHU, C.-H., MULLEN, T. & PENNOCK, D. M. Information markets vs. opinion pools: an empirical comparison. Proceedings of the 6th ACM Conference on Electronic commerce, 2005 Vancouver, BC, Canada. 58-67.

CHRISTIANSEN, J. D. 2007. Prediction Markets: Practical Experiments in Small Markets and Behaviours Observed *Journal of Prediction Markets,* 1, 17-41.

CLAR, G. 2003. Forecasting Options for the Future - to Gain Foresight to Select and Shape Them. *Journal of Forecasting,* 22, 83-91.

COOPER, G. 2001. *Winning at New Products. Accelerating the process from idea to launch,* Cambridge, MA, Perseus.

COWAN, G. 1998. *Statistical Data Analysis* Oxford University Press.

COWGILL, B., WOLFERS, J. & ZITZEWITZ, E. 2008. Using Prediction Markets to Track Information Flows: Evidence from Google. *Working Paper.*

CUHLS, K. 2003. From Forecasting to Foresight Processes - New Participative Foresight Activities in Germany. *Journal of Forecasting,* 22, 93-111.

DAHAN, E., SOUKHOROUKOVA, A. & SPANN, M. 2007. Preference Markets: Organizing Securities Markets for Opinion Surveys with Infinite Scalability. *Working Paper, University of California Los Angeles.*

DAHAN, E., SOUKHOROUKOVA, A. & SPANN, M. 2009. New Product Development 2.0: Preference Markets. How Scalable Securities Markets Identify Winning Product Concepts & Attributes. *Journal of Product Innovation Management,* forthcoming.

DEBNATH, S., PENNOCK, D. M., GILES, C. L. & LAWRENCE, S. Information incorporation in online in-Game sports betting markets. Proceedings of the 4th ACM conference on Electronic commerce 2003 San Diego, CA, USA. ACM Press, 258-259.

DOLFSMA, W. 2004. The process of new service development – issues of formalization and approbability. *Report Series Research in Management.*

ERIKSON, R. S. & WLEZIEN, C. Are Political Markets Really Superior to Polls as Election Predictors? Annual Meeting of the Midwest Political Science Association, 2006 Chicago.

FAMA, E. F. 1970a. Efficient Capital Markets: A Review of Theory and Empirical Work. *Journal of Finance,* 25, 383-417.

FAMA, E. F. 1970b. Efficient capital markets: A review of theory and empirical work. *Journal of Finance,* 25, 383-417.

FAMA, E. F. 1991. Efficient Capital Markets: II. *Journal of Finance,* 46, 1575-1617.

FIGLEWSKI, S. 1979. Subjective Information and Market Efficiency in a Betting Model. *Journal of Political Economy,* 87, 75-88.

FILZMAIER, P., BEYRL, M., HAUSER, F. & HUBER, J. 2003. Wahlbörsen als interdisziplinäres Instrument der Sozialforschung. *SWS Rundschau,* 3, 387-410.

FORREST, D., GODDARD, J. & SIMMONS, R. 2005. Odds-setters as forecasters: The case of English football. *International Journal of Forecasting,* 21, 551-564.

FORSYTHE, R., FRANK, M., KRISHNAMURTHY, V. & ROSS, T. W. 1995. Using Market Prices to Predict Election Results: The 1993 UBC Election Stock Market. *The Canadian Journal of Economics* 28, 770-793.

FORSYTHE, R., FRANK, M., KRISHNAMURTHY, V. & ROSS, T. W. 1998. Markets as Predictors of Election Outcomes: Campaign Events and Judgment Bias in the 1993 UBC Election Stock Market. *Canadian Public Policy,* 24.

FORSYTHE, R., NELSON, F., NEUMANN, G. & WRIGHT, J. 1992. Anatomy of an Experimental Political Stock Market. *American Economic Review,* 82, 1142-1161.

FORSYTHE, R., NELSON, F., NEUMANN, G. & WRIGHT, J. 1994. The 1992 Iowa Political Stock Market: September Forecasts. *The Political Methodologist,* 5, 15-19.

FORSYTHE, R., RIETZ, T. A. & ROSS, T. 1999. Wishes, expectations and actions: a survey on price formation in election stock markets. *Journal of Economic Behavior and Organization,* 39, 83-110.

FOUTZ, N. Z. & JANK, W. 2010. Prerelease Demand Forecasting for Motion Pictures Using Functional Shape Analysis of Virtual Stock Markets. *Marketing Science,* 29, 568-579.

FOWLER, J. H. 2006. Elections and Markets: The Effect of Partisanship, Policy Risk, and Electoral Margins on the Economy. *The Journal of Politics,* 68, 89-103.

FRANKE, M., GEYER-SCHULZ, A. & HOSER, B. 2005. Analyzing Trading Behavior in Transaction Data of Electronic Election Markets. *In:* BAIER, D., DECKER, R. & SCHMIDT-THIEME, L. (eds.) *Data Analysis and Decision Support.* Springer.

FRANKE, M., GEYER-SCHULZ, A. & HOSER, B. 2006. On the Analysis of Asymmetric Directed Communication Structures in Electronic Election Markets. *In:* BILLARI, F. C., FENT, T., PRSKAWETZ, A. & SCHEFFRAN, J. (eds.) *Agent-Based Computational Modelling.* Physica.

FRANKE, M., HOSER, B. & SCHRÖDER, J. 2008. On the Analysis of Irregular Stock Market Trading Behaviour. *In:* PREISACH, C., BURKHARDT, H., SCHMIDT-THIEME, L. & DECKER, R. (eds.) *Data Analysis, Machine Learning, and Applications.* Spinger.

GANDAR, J. M., DARE, W. H., BROWN, C. R. & ZUBER, R. A. 1998. Informed Traders and Price Variations in the Betting Market for Professional Basketball Games. *Journal of Finance,* 53, 385-401.

GELERNTER, D., CARRIERIO, N. & CHANDRAN, S. 1985. Parallel Processing in Linda. *International Conference on Parallel Processing.*

GEYER-SCHULZ, A., LUCKNER, S., SCHRÖDER, J., SKIERA, B., SLAMKA, C. & WEINHARDT, C. 2007. Empirical Evaluation of Call Auctions in Prediction Markets. Working Paper, Universität Karlsruhe (TH).

GLOSTEN, L. R. & MILGROM, P. R. 1985. Bid, Ask and Transaction Prices in a Specialist Market With Heterogeneously Informed Traders. *Journal of Financial Economics,* 14, 71-100.

GOLDENBERG, J., LEHMANN, D. R. & MAZURSKY, D. 2001. The Idea Itself and the Circumstances of Its Emergence as Predictors of New Product Success. *Management Science,* 47, 69-84.

GRAEFE, A. & WEINHARDT, C. 2008. Long-term Forecasting with Prediction Markets - A Field Experiment on Applicability and Expert Confidence. *Journal of Prediction Markets,* 2, 71-92.

GRIFFIN, A. 1997. PDMA research on new product development practices: updating trends and benchmarking best practices. *Journal of Product Innovation Management,* 14, 429-458.

GRUCA, T. S., BERG, J. E. & CIPRIANO, M. 2003. The Effect of Electronic Markets on Forecasts of New Product Success. *Information Systems Frontiers,* 5, 95-105.

GÜRKAYNAK, R. S. & WOLFERS, J. 2006. Macroeconomic derivatives: an initial analysis of market-based macro forecasts, uncertainty, and risk. *In:* PISSARIDES, C. & FRANKEL, J. (eds.) *NBER International Seminar on Macroeconomics.* MIT Press.

HAHN, B. & TETLOCK, P. (eds.) 2006. *Information Markets: A New Way of Making Decisions*: AEI-Brookings Press.

HANSEN, J., SCHMIDT, C. & STROBEL, M. 2004. Manipulation in Political Stock Markets - Preconditions and Evidence. *Applied Economics Letters,* 11, 459-463.

HANSON, R. Could Gambling Save Science? Encouraging an Honest Consensus. Proceedings of the Eighth International Conference on Risk and Gambling, 1990a London.

HANSON, R. 1990b. Market-Based Foresight: A Proposal. *Foresight Update,* 10, 1-4.

HANSON, R. 1992. Idea Futures: Encouraging an Honest Consensus. *Extropy,* 3, 7-17.

HANSON, R. 1999. Decision Markets. *IEEE Intelligent Systems,* 14, 16-19.

HANSON, R. 2003. Combinatorial Information Market Design. *Information Systems Frontiers,* 5, 105-119.

HANSON, R. 2006. Foul Play in Information Markets. *In:* HAHN, R. & TETLOCK, P. C. (eds.) *Information Markets: A New Way of Making Decisions in the Public and Private Sectors.* Washington D.C.: AEI Press.

HANSON, R. 2007. Logarithmic Market Scoring Rules for Modular Combinatorial Information Aggregation. *Journal of Prediction Markets,* 1, 3-15.

HANSON, R., OPREA, R. & PORTER, D. 2006. Information Aggregation and Manipulation in an Experimental Market. *Journal of Economic Behavior and Organization,* 60, 449-459.

HARRISON, G. W., LAU, M. I. & RUTSTRÖM, E. E. 2007. Estimating Risk Attitudes in Denmark: A Field Experiment. *Scandinavian Journal of Economics,* 109, 341-368.

HAYEK, F. 1945. The Use of Knowledge in Society. *American Economic Review,* 35, 519-530.

HOLT, C. A. & LAURY, S. K. 2002. Risk Aversion and Incentive Effects. *American Economic Review,* 92, 1644-1655.

HOLT, C. A. & LAURY, S. K. 2005. Risk Aversion and Incentive Effects: New Data Without Order Effects. *American Economic Review,* 95, 902-912.

HUBER, J. & HAUSER, F. Systematic mispricing in experimental markets – evidence from political stock markets. Proceedings of the International Conference on Finance, 2005 Kopenhagen, Denmark.

JACOBSEN, B., POTTERS, J., SCHRAM, A., VAN WINDEN, F. & WIT, J. 2000. (In)accuracy of a European political stock market: The influence of common value structures - Ambiguity and competence in choice under uncertainty *European Economic Review,* 44, 205-230.

JANA, R. 2007. Service Innovation: The Next Big Thing. *Business Week*, 29.03.2007.

JENSEN, M. C. 1978. Some Anomalous Evidence Regarding Market Efficiency. *Journal of Financial Economics,* 6, 95-101.

KIVIAT, B. 2004. The End of Management? *Time,* 164.

KOU, S. G. & SOBEL, M. E. 2004. Forecasting the Vote: A Theoretical Comparison of Election Markets and Public Opinion Polls. *Political Analysis,* 12, 277-295.

LACOMB, C. A., BARNETT, J. A. & PAN, Q. 2007. The Imagination Market. *Information Systems Frontiers,* 9, 245-256.

LUCKNER, S. Price Formation in Sports Prediction Markets – A Cross-Cultural Study. *In:* KERSTEN, G. E., RIOS, J. & CHEN, E., eds. Group Decision and Negotiation (GDN) 2007, 2007 Montreal, Canada. 210-212.

LUCKNER, S., SCHRÖDER, J. & SLAMKA, C. 2007. On the Forecast Accuracy of Sports Prediction Markets. *In:* GIMPEL, H., JENNINGS, N. R., KERSTEN, G., OCKENFELS, A. & WEINHARDT , C. (eds.) *Negotiation and Market Engineering.* LNBIP 2, Springer.

LUCKNER, S. & WEINHARDT, C. 2007. How to Pay Traders in Information Markets? Results from a Field Experiment. *Journal of Prediction Markets,* 1, 147-156.

MADHAVAN, A. 1992. Trading Mechanisms in Securities Markets. *Journal of Finance,* 47, 607-641.

MALONEY, M. & MULHERIN, H. 2003. The Complexity of Price Discovery in an Efficient Market: The Stock Market Reaction to the Challenger Crash. *Journal of Corporate Finance,* 9, 453-479.

MANGOLD, B., DOOLEY, M., FLAKE, G. W., HOFFMAN, H., KASTURI, T., PENNOCK, D. M. & DORNFEST, R. 2005. The Tech Buzz Game. *Computer,* 38, 94-97.

MANN, H. B. & WHITNEY, D. R. 1947. On a test of whether one of two random variables is stochastically larger than the other. *Annals of Mathematical Statistics,* 18, 50-60.

MCKELVEY, R. D. & PAGE, T. 1990. Public and Private Information: An Experimental Study of Information Pooling. *Econometrica,* 58, 1321-1339.

NEEDLY, A. D. Servitization of Manufacturing. 14th European Operations Management Association Conference, 2007 Ankara, Turkey.

NOHRIA, N. & STEWART, T. A. 2006. Risk, Uncertainty, and Doubt. *Harvard Business Review,* 84, 39-40.

OLIVEN, K. & RIETZ, T. A. 2004. Suckers Are Born but Markets Are Made: Individual Rationality, Arbitrage, and Market Efficiency on an Electronic Futures Market. *Management Science,* 50, 336-351.

ORTNER, G. 1997. Forecasting Markets - An Industrial Application: Part I. Working Paper, TU Vienna.

ORTNER, G. 2000. Aktienmärkte als Industrielles Vorhersagemodell. *Zeitschrift für Betriebswirtschaft (ZfB) - Ergänzungsheft,* 70, 115-125.

ORTNER, G., STEPAN, A. & ZECHNER, J. 1995. Political Stock Markets - The Austrian Experiences. *Zeitschrift für Betriebswirtschaft (ZfB),* Ergänzungsheft 4/95, 123-135.

PENNOCK, D. M. A Dynamic Pari-Mutuel Market for Hedging, Wagering, and Information Aggregation. ACM Conference on Electronic Commerce 2004, 2004 New York, USA. 170-179.

PENNOCK, D. M., LAWRENCE, S., GILES, C. L. & NIELSEN, F. A. 2000. The Power of Play: Efficiency and Forecast Accuracy of Web Market Games. *Technical Report 2000-168.* Princeton: NEC Research Institute.

PENNOCK, D. M., LAWRENCE, S., NIELSEN, F. A. & GILES, C. L. Extracting collective probabilistic forecasts from web games. Proceedings of the 7th ACM SIGKDD International Conference on Knowledge Discovery and Data Mining 2001a San Francisco, CA, USA. 174-183.

PENNOCK, D. M., LAWRENCE, S., NIELSEN, F. A. & GILES, C. L. 2001b. The real power of artificial markets. *Science,* 291, 987-988.

PENNOCK, D. M. & SAMI, R. 2007. Computational Aspects of Prediction Market. *In:* NISAN, N., ROUGHGARDEN, T., TARDOS, E. & VAZIRANI, V. V. (eds.) *Algorithmic Game Theory.* New York: Cambridge University Press.

PLOTT, C. R. 2000. Markets as Information Gathering Tools. *Southern Economic Journal,* 67, 1-15.

PLOTT, C. R. & SUNDER, S. 1982. Efficiency of experimental security markets with insider information: An application of rational expectations models. *Journal of Political Economy,* 90, 663-698.

PLOTT, C. R. & SUNDER, S. 1988. Rational Expectations and the Aggregation of Diverse Information in Laboratory Security Markets. *Econometrica,* 56, 1085-1118.

POLGREEN, P. M., NELSON, F. D. & NEUMANN, G. R. 2007. Use of Prediction Markets to Forecast Infectious Disease Activity. *Clinical Infectious Diseases,* 44, 272-279.

POPE, P. F. & PEEL, D. A. 1989. Information, Prices and Efficiency in a Fixed-Odds Betting Market. *Economica,* 56, 323-341.

RADA, J. & VANDERMERWE, S. 1988. Servitization of business: adding value by adding service. *European Management Journal,* 6, 314-320.

ROCHFORD, L. 1991. Generating and screening new product ideas. *Industrial Marketing Management,* 20, 287-296.

ROLL, R. 1984. Orange Juice and Weather. *American Economic Review,* 74, 861-880.

ROSENBLOOM, E. S. & NOTZ, W. W. 2006. Statistical Tests of Real-Money versus Play-Money Prediction Markets. *Electronic Markets - The International Journal* 16.

SALO, A. & CUHLS, K. 2003. Technology foresight—past and future. *Journal of Forecasting,* 22, 79-82.

SCHMIDT, C. & WERWATZ, A. 2002. How well do markets predict the outcome of an event? The Euro 2000 soccer championships experiment. *Discussion Papers on*

Strategic Interaction Jena, Germany: Max Planck Institute for Research into Economic Systems.

SCHÖNFELDINGER, W. J. 1996. *Kooperation und Kommunikation in heterogenen Rechner- und Sprachumgebungen mit Perl-Linda.* Wirtschaftsuniversität.

SCHRÖDER, J. 2009. *Manipulations in Prediction Markets - Analysis of Trading Behaviour not Conforming with Trading Regulations,* Karlsruhe, Universitätsverlag Karlsruhe.

SERVAN-SCHREIBER, E., WOLFERS, J., PENNOCK, D. & GALEBACH, B. 2004. Prediction Markets: Does Money Matter? *Electronic Markets - The International Journal,* 14, 243-251.

SKIERA, B. & SPANN, M. 2004. Opportunities of Virtual Stock Markets to Support New Product Development. *In:* ALBERS, S. (ed.) *Cross-functional Innovation Management.* Wiesbaden: Gabler.

SLAMKA, C., JANK, W. & SKIERA, B. 2009a. Second-Generation Prediction Markets for Information Aggregation: A Comparison of Payoff Mechanisms. *Forthcoming at the Journal of Forecasting.*

SLAMKA, C., SKIERA, B. & SPANN, M. 2009b. A Simulative Comparison of Automated Markets Makers in Prediction Markets. *Working Paper, Goethe-University Frankfurt.*

SLAMKA, C., SOUKHOROUKOVA, A. & SPANN, M. 2008. Event Studies in Play- and Real Money Prediction Market. *Journal of Prediction Markets,* 2, 53-70.

SMITH, A. M., FISCHBACHER, M. & WILSON, F. A. 2007. New Service Development: From Panoramas to Precision. *European Management Journal,* 25, 370-383.

SMITH, M. A., PATON, D. & WILLIAMS, L. V. 2006. Market Efficiency in Person-to-Person Betting *Economica,* 73, 673-689.

SNYDER, W. W. 1978. Horse Racing: Testing the Efficient Markets Model. *Journal of Finance,* 33, 1109-1118.

SOUKHOROUKOVA, A. & SPANN, M. 2005. New Product Development with Internet-based Information Markets: Theory and Empirical Application. *13th European Conference on Information Systems (ECIS).*

SOUKHOROUKOVA, A., SPANN, M. & SKIERA, B. 2009. Creating and Evaluating New Product Ideas with Idea Markets. Working Paper, University of Passau.

SOUKHOROUKOVA, A., SPANN, M. & SKIERA, B. 2010. Generating and Evaluating New Product Ideas with Idea Markets. *Jounal of Product Innovation,* forthcoming.

SOUKHOROUKOVA, A., SPANN, M. & SKIERA, B. 2011. Sourcing, Filtering, and Evaluating New Product Ideas: An Empirical Exploration of the Performance of Idea Markets. *Journal of Product Innovation*, forthcoming.

SPANN, M., ERNST, H., SKIERA, B. & SOLL, J. H. 2009. Identification of Lead Users for Consumer Products via Virtual Stock Markets. *Journal of Product Innovation Management,* 26, 322-335.

SPANN, M. & SKIERA, B. 2003. Internet-Based Virtual Stock Markets for Business Forecasting. *Management Science,* 49, 1310-1326.

SPANN, M. & SKIERA, B. 2009. Sports Forecasting: A Comparison of the Forecast Accuracy of Prediction Markets, Betting Odds and Tipsters. *Journal of Forecasting,* 28, 55-72.

STATHEL, S., LUCKNER, S., TESCHNER, F., WEINHARDT, C., REESON, A. & WHITTEN, S. AKX – An Exchange for Predicting Water Dam Levels in Australia. ITEE 09, 2009.

THALER, R. & ZIEMBA, W. 1988. Parimutuel Betting Markets: Racetracks and Lotteries. *Journal of Economic Perspectives,* 2, 161-174.

TZIRALIS, G. & TATSIOPOULOS, I. 2007a. Prediction Markets: An Extended Literature Review. *Journal of Prediction Markets,* 1, 75-91.

TZIRALIS, G. & TATSIOPOULOS, I. 2007b. Prediction markets: an information aggregation perspective to the forecasting problem. *World Review of Entrepreneurship, Management and Sustainable Development,* 3, 251-259.

VAN BRUGGEN, G. H., SPANN, M., LILIEN, G. L. & SKIERA, B. 2006. Institutional Forecasting: The Performance of Thin Virtual Stock Markets. *ERIM Report Series Reference No. ERS-2006-028-MKT.* Rotterdam: Erasmus Research Institute of Management (ERIM).

VLASTAKIS, N., DOTSIS, G. & MARKELOS, R. N. Beating the Odds: Arbitrage and Winning Strategies in the European Football Betting Market. European Financial Management Association Annual Meeting, 2006 Madrid, Spain.

WEINHARDT, C., HOLTMANN, C. & NEUMANN, D. 2003. Market Engineering. *Wirtschaftsinformatik,* 45, 635-640.

WEINHARDT, C., NEUMANN, D. & HOLTMANN, C. 2006a. Computer-aided Market Engineering *Communications of the ACM,* 49, 79.

WEINHARDT, C., VAN DINTHER, C., GRUNENBERG, M., KOLITZ, K., KUNZELMANN, M., MÄKIÖ, J., WEBER, I. & WELTZIEN, H. 2006b. *CAME-Toolsuite meet2trade - auf dem Weg zum Computer Aided Market Engineering,* Karlsruhe, Universitätsverlag Karlsruhe.

WEINHARDT, C., VAN DINTHER, C., KOLITZ, K., MÄKIÖ, J. & WEBER, I. meet2trade: A generic electronic trading platform. 4th Workshop on e-Business (WEB 2005), 2005 Las Vegas, USA.

WOLFERS, J. & ZITZEWITZ, E. 2004. Prediction Markets. *Journal of Economic Perspectives,* 18, 107-126.

WOLFERS, J. & ZITZEWITZ, E. 2006. Interpreting Prediction Market Prices as Probabilities. NBER Working Paper No. 12200.

WOODLAND, L. M. & WOODLAND, B. M. 1994. Market Efficiency and the Favorite-Longshot Bias: The Baseball Betting Market. *Journal of Finance,* 49, 269-279.

FSC
www.fsc.org
MIX
Papier | Fördert gute Waldnutzung
FSC® C083411

Kolibri 360 GmbH
Ferdinand-Jühlke-Straße 7
99095 Erfurt, Deutschland
produktsicherheit@kolibri360.de